A Multiple Intelligences Road To

A QUALITY CLASSROOM

Sally Berman

SkyLight

TRAINING AND PUBLISHING, INC.

Arlington Heights, Illinois

A Multiple Intelligences Road to a Quality Classroom

Published by IRI/SkyLight Training and Publishing, Inc.
2626 S. Clearbrook Drive, Arlington Heights, Illinois 60005-5310
800-348-4474, 847-290-6600
FAX 847-290-6609
info@iriskylight. com
http://www.iriskylight.com

Creative Director: Robin Fogarty
Managing Editor: Julia Noblitt
Editor: Monica Phillips
Proofreader: Troy Slocum
Graphic Designer: Bruce Leckie
Cover and Illustration Designer: David Stockman
Junior Designer: Heidi Ray
Type Compositor: Donna Ramirez
Production Supervisor: Bob Crump

Library of Congress Catalog Card Number 95-79276
ISBN 1-57517-005-1

1594C-7-97-V
Item Number 1346
06 05 04 03 02 01 00 99 98 97   15 14 13 12 11 10 9 8 7 6 5 4 3

To Quality, the goal that keeps us growing, and to Al,
my partner and friend on the road.

Contents

• Part III •

Following the Road to Success

Self-Evaluating and Planning for Quality Learning

Acknowledgments

I gratefully acknowledge the following people: Nancy Robb, principal of Palatine High School in Palatine, Illinois, who offered me the training that led to this collection of strategies; Dr. William Glasser, who wrote the books, spoke on the videotapes, and made the in-person visits that gave me the control theory information; Jeanette McDaniel, who interpreted the words in those books, provided the experiences that led to my better understanding of them, modeled effective personal control, and left me alone to feel frustrated, angry, and finally elated about the reorganization of my total behavior—my internalization of control theory; and Diane Gossen, who helped me stretch and flex those newly developed control theory muscles.

In addition, Leslee Johnson, Ken Spengler, Jane Merydith, Jerry O'Brien, Darlene Hahnfeld, Marilyn Morel, and Bob Schuetz shared ideas, role-played, encouraged, and celebrated with me in good times. They also stayed with me through the uneasiness and occasional anger of reorganization. Working with them helped me find new comfort zones, vast resources of personal energy, and more effective control of my life.

Above all, my students have contributed invaluable inspiration for this book. As they learned control theory, many things changed in the classroom. They admitted that blaming others or making excuses got in the way of improvement, and they gained more effective control of their behaviors. I felt the need to question behaviors less and less often. The students tackled the tasks of self-evaluating, setting goals, and developing plans to improve the quality of their learning. Their best thoughts and mine combined to produce the quality learning roadmap found in chapter 5. Their written comments to me expressed their pride in owning their accomplishments and their relief that an adult actually realized that (1) she could not tell them how to learn and (2) learning is an individual process that each individual has his or her own most effective way of doing. Arguments about grades ceased—each student knew exactly what grade he or she was earning and what he or she could do to improve it. Students focused on learning, not grades. The quality of learning improved dramatically.

Finally, my husband, Al, drove me to class, participated in role-plays at home, helped me hone my control theory understanding and my reality therapy skills, and encouraged me to write this book. As I developed materials, I kept saying, "I think there's a book in here somewhere." Al would answer, "Well, someday it will come out and announce itself." When that happened, he encouraged me to set everything else aside so that I could get it written.

My thanks to all of these special people. They all helped me find the information, time, energy, and inspiration to get this job done.

Introduction

I have talked with many teachers who have participated in basic intensive weeks, become very excited about control theory and Dr. William Glasser's quality school ideas, and then asked, "So what do we do next? Where do we go from here?" You may have the same questions. You may be having trouble designing lessons that will help your students learn control theory and become more effective learners. This book contains twenty-one activities or strategies that I have used with students to help them develop and organize some new learning behaviors.

The Quality School

At this point, you may be thinking, "I think I've heard about Dr. William Glasser and his quality school ideas, but I'm not certain that I remember what those ideas are." Here is a quick review of (or introduction to) those ideas. A quality school is a quality work and study place. The administrators and teachers lead and manage; they do not boss. They convince students that doing quality schoolwork will add value to their lives. Students do their work because they see that learning is useful and fun. Teachers take time to show students that the work they are being asked to do is useful—that it will add meaning to their lives or give them lifelong skills. Teachers and administrators model the behaviors that they ask students to use. Coercion is not used to "manage" students—students are taught to self-evaluate their behaviors and to choose effective behaviors. Students also self-evaluate the quality of their schoolwork. They are asked, "Is this the best work that you can do right now? How can it be improved? Do you need help in discovering how to do better in school (and in life)?" Students are told that there is only one rule in the school—courtesy. They are told that the people in the school believe in treating others with courtesy—that they believe in respecting and helping others. Teachers and administrators believe that almost all students are capable of doing quality schoolwork—and they share this belief with students.

Teachers are viewed as professionals, so they are not evaluated using standard evaluation instruments and procedures. Instead, teachers are asked to self-evaluate. They are asked, "What are you doing that is quality work? What are you doing that is the best work you can do to enhance student learning and be a successful classroom manager? What do you want to strengthen? What help do you need? Who do you want to help you?" Most importantly, all administrators, teachers, students, and parents are taught control theory. This gives them a common vocabulary and viewpoint that can be used to strengthen the entire school.

Control Theory

Control theory was developed by Glasser to explain why all living organisms (including people) behave. Developed as an alternative to stimulus-response thinking, Glasser's control theory states all we can do is behave, and we choose our own behaviors. We behave to control our input—to get what we want. Glasser calls the collection of wants that each of us accumulates our *quality world*. We behave if we want a picture from our quality world, but sometimes we do not get it. Our frustration in not getting what we want initiates a total behavior that may or may not be effective, but it is the best behavior we know at the time. If we can learn new behaviors, we give ourselves more ways to get our quality world pictures. The more flexible we are, the more "in control" we feel. We do not react to outside stimuli—we choose our behaviors because our wants help us meet one or more of five basic needs. These needs are survival, belonging, power, freedom, and fun. Our needs are not equally strong—some needs are stronger and others are weaker—and are often in conflict with one another. A behavior that gives us more freedom, like skydiving, may frustrate another need—in this case, survival. All behaviors are total and are made up of four parts—acting, thinking, feeling, and physiology. We are always aware of how we feel and of whether that feeling is pleasant or painful. Our actions and thinking can affect our feeling and physiology. Although we cannot control others, we may be able to influence them if we help them meet one or more of their basic needs. Teachers who want more background in control theory are encouraged to read *Control Theory* or *Control Theory in the Classroom,* both by Dr. William Glasser.

Multiple Intelligences

The lessons in this book have been developed to use the multiple intelligences identified by Howard Gardner and his associates. Both Gardner and Glasser believe that a key component of an intelligence is the ability to create and solve new problems and that new learning results from defining and resolving new problems or challenges. Glasser states that a reward for new learning is *fun,* which is one of the five basic needs that all people have. Glasser and Gardner also believe that intelligences can be strengthened and developed with support, encouragement, and practice. They believe that people who are willing to work at problem solving and who are given opportunities to do so will become "more intelligent."

According to Gardner and his associates, we all have (at least) seven intelligences. Students demonstrate their use of those intelligences in a variety of ways. A student who likes to work with others, belongs to several clubs or athletic teams, or is more interested in learning about people behind the scenes than learning about abstract theories demonstrates a high comfort level with *interpersonal/social* intelligence. Activities that are done with partners or in cooperative groups give students experiences in this intelligence.

A student who likes to write in his journal, set individual goals, do some personal thinking and planning before joining a group, read silently, and feel in control of his or her own learning demonstrates a highly developed *intrapersonal/introspective* intelligence. Reflective journal writing, before-class preparation, goal-setting, planning, and self-evaluation use and strengthen the intrapersonal intelligence.

A student who sings as she walks into the room, taps her pencil or foot rhythmically, hums along with the soundtrack in the movie, loves (and perhaps writes) poetry, or remembers advertising chants shows a highly developed *musical/rhythmic* intelligence. Inventing cheers and chants, writing poems or song verses, and using favorite pieces of music to reinforce learning help students flex their musical/rhythmic muscles.

A student who fills his notebook with doodles and sketches, comments on the charts and pictures that decorate the room, notices when those charts and pictures are different, loves graphic organizers, and always wants to use the teacher's colored markers is very comfortable with his or her *visual/spatial* intelligence. Activities that ask students to generate graphics or use graphic organizers and activities in which the teacher uses newsprint to record ideas from a whole-class discussion give visual/spatial experiences.

A student who clicks her pen; swings her foot or taps her pencil (but not necessarily in a rhythmic way); is an accomplished cook, athlete, seamstress, potter, or mechanic; or enjoys working with models or other manipulatives has a highly developed *bodily/kinesthetic* intelligence. Activities that ask students to invent hand signals and "act out" information or those that encourage students to move around the room use the bodily/kinesthetic intelligence.

A student who speaks clearly and to the point, loves reading and writing assignments, or belongs to the drama club, the school newspaper, or yearbook—a student who seems to mirror the learning style of many of the teachers you know—has a very well-developed *verbal/linguistic* intelligence. Writing and discussion activities allow students to use the verbal/linguistic intelligence. (Glasser believes that teaching students to write well is one of the most useful things we can do in school because writing is a lifelong skill.)

A student who is a "computer nerd" or a "science freak" is usually associated with a highly developed *logical/mathematical* intelligence—but there is more to the picture. Activities that ask students to use Venn diagrams and grids to organize information or make story boards to sequence information, or activities that ask students to prioritize (think of several examples and then pick your favorite), also involve the logical/mathematical intelligence.

The activities in this book use all seven intelligences to help students feel more comfortable in the classroom. If classroom activities integrate all seven intelligences—in particular, if the bodily/kinesthetic, musical/rhythmic, and visual/spatial intelligences are regularly used—most discipline problems evaporate! When we ignore the use of those intelligences, we are ignoring the intelligences of highest comfort for one-third of our students.

Overview of the Book

To use this book in developing your own quality classroom with multiple intelligences, browse through the entire book first. That way you will become more familiar with the layout of the chapters and may decide on a series of lessons to use. I recommend starting with trust-building activities (part 1), moving on to control theory (part 2), and then doing quality learning (part 3). Some teachers have been tempted to skip control theory, but I have found that students are better self-evaluators and goal setters if they understand some control theory basics. You may also discover that you want to repeat some of the lessons during the course of one school year. I ask students to use the control theory track (chapter 4) very often to analyze their own effective control. I personally cycle through the activities in part 3 continuously and encourage students to do the same. I find that frequent self-evaluation and goal revising promote the best learning.

Each lesson is divided into three parts. "Getting on the Road" contains some introductory information and/or the rationale for doing the activity and gives a frontload, or "hook," activity that can be used with students to set up the lesson. "Cruising the Road" is a set of step-by-step instructions for actually doing the lesson with students. Look for the sidebar note that identifies which of Howard Gardner's multiple intelligences are targeted in the activity and how students will be using them. "Stopping to Think" contains suggestions for processing the lesson or providing closure, usually a writing exercise in the students' personal journals. As Thomas Dewey said, "We do not learn from our experiences; we learn from processing our experiences." I encourage students to use prose, poetry, sketches, and song lyrics in their journal entries.

I have found the activities in this book to be very useful in establishing the conditions for quality and promoting mastery learning with students in my classroom. Using these lessons does take time away from subject-matter content. I believe that helping students become better learners is a fair trade-off for deleting some content that they may very likely forget anyway. I also believe that by giving students a better understanding of control theory and helping them use the tools that lead to mastery learning, I am helping them develop useful, lifelong skills. Newspaper and television news stories suggest to me that people need to learn how to be in more effective control of their lives. Teachers who include control theory in their classroom agendas provide students with tools they can use to become responsible, effective adults.

• Part I •

Paving the Road

Setting the Environment for Quality

Roadwork Ahead

Three Trust Builders

Activity #1

Basic Trust Builder

Getting on the Road

This trust-building activity is a good icebreaker for the first day of class because it is done in pairs. Assigning partners, rather than asking the students to choose, provides for a nice mix and helps foster the perception that everyone is equally important in the classroom.

Introduce yourself to your students and let them know you believe that establishing a trusting environment in the classroom is vitally important. (See *The Quality School Teacher* by William Glasser for tips on self-disclosing on the first day of school.) Tell them that this activity is designed to help them get to know their classmates. Emphasize that people begin to trust others once they get to know them.

Cruising the Road

In this activity, students use their **verbal/linguistic** intelligence to interview each other. They use their **interpersonal/social** intelligence to work with their partners.

1. Instruct the students that they will be doing a focus interview with a partner and then introducing their partners to the rest of the class using the information they learned.

2. Ask the students how they will remember their partners' information. Record a short list of their ideas on the blackboard or on chart paper.

3. Hand out the interview questions. (Some suggested focus questions are included at the end of this activity.) Model the interview by telling the students your information as you go over the questions.

4. Tell the students that they will each have two minutes to interview their partners.

5. Ask the students to describe what they will be doing. Call on students at random to review the instructions.

6. Ask them to use quiet voices during the interviews. Tell them that quiet voices will help everyone hear what their partners are saying and will help them hear you give the time signals. Ask them what these quiet voices will sound like and look like. Record a few of their ideas on the board or on chart paper.

7. Quickly assign partners. One good way to do this is to have the students number off. (For example, if there are twenty-four students, you will have twelve pairs. Have the students number off by twelves.) Tell the partners to move close together. When all of the students have finished moving, signal the start of the activity. Announce the end of the first two minutes (when it is time to end the first interview and begin the second). Announce the end of the activity.

8. Ask the students if they want you to call on pairs for the introductions or if pairs want to volunteer. Be certain that every pair participates in the introductions. Encourage and model good listening by focusing on the introductions as they are given.

9. Ask partners to shake hands and thank each other at the conclusion of the introductions.

IRI/Skylight Training and Publishing, Inc.

FOCUS QUESTIONS

1. What's in a name?

   First, ask your partner where he or she went to school last year. Then ask the following:

   - Do you know why your parents chose your name?
   - Is there some interesting meaning or family history behind the selection of your name?
   - Do you know of any historical or fictional characters who have had your name?
   - Have you ever wished you had a different name? What is it?
   - Have you had any interesting experiences because of your name?

   (High school teachers may want their students to include these additional questions: Where are you before this class? Where do you go next? When do you have lunch?)

2. What will you be?

   First, ask your partner where he or she went to school last year. Then ask the following questions:

   - What do you want to be when you grow up?
   - What focused your interest on that career?
   - What kind of training/education do you need for that career?
   - Where do you plan on getting that training?

   (High school teachers may want their students to include these additional questions: Where are you before this class? Where do you go next? When do you have lunch?)

3. What do you like?

   First, ask your partner where he or she went to school last year. Then ask these questions:

   - What is your favorite music? Sport? Television show? Food? Color? Weather? Season? Holiday? Pet?
   - What do you like to do with your free time?
   - Do you like to get up early in the morning?
   - Do you like to stay up late at night?

   (High school teachers may want their students to include these additional questions: Where are you before this class? Where do you go next? When do you have lunch?)

   Compare notes after the interviews to find ways in which you are alike.

Stopping to Think

Ask the students to self-evaluate by writing answers to these questions in a personal journal: As an interviewer, what were my best actions? What were my best thoughts? What skills would I like to strengthen next time? Do I want any help in strengthening my skills? Who do I see helping me? How comfortable am I when I use my verbal and social intelligences? How can I get more practice using those intelligences?

Activity #2

Intermediate Trust Builder

Getting on the Road

To establish a trusting atmosphere in the classroom, the students need many opportunities early in the year to work together on activities that allow them to get acquainted. This is particularly important in a large school where the students may not have been assigned to classes together in the past. This activity will take some students out of their comfort zones, so I recommend it as a second trust-building activity. It is done in groups of three. Because these groups will be kept together for awhile, assign the students to groups that are as heterogeneous as possible. Each group needs a big sheet of chart paper, colored markers, and masking tape.

Tell the students that you are asking them to find out more about each other and design a graphic that will show what they have learned. Tell them that the people they work with today will be their teammates for a while (I keep these groups together for about nine weeks). This activity involves more risk for students who feel uncomfortable when asked to draw. I help them feel more at ease by saying, "I know that some of you are thinking to yourself, 'I can't draw!' Well, I (pointing to myself) can't either! Many of your classmates probably feel that way too! I'll bet we can all do stick figures and smiley faces—and even daisies! Just do your best. If you sketch lightly in pencil first and then color in your graphic with marker, you may be more satisfied with the result. You may also find that one of your teammates can draw. Above all, try to remember that what we're after is a graphic, not great art."

Cruising the Road

In this activity, students use their **visual/ spatial** intelligence to design a team crest and their **interpersonal/ social** intelligence to perform their roles as members of small groups.

1. Tell the students that they will be working in groups of three. Their job will be to find five ways in which the three of them are alike and one way in which each of them is unique.

2. Ask the students for ideas about what topics they may want to explore as they look for commonalities. Contribute a few ideas to start the list (i.e., Was everyone in the group born here? What color of eyes does each teammate have? Is everyone athletic? Does everyone like snow?) Record a list of ideas on the board or on chart paper.

3. Tell the students that each group will have a recorder to write down a list of their ideas, a conductor to pick up the materials and encourage the group to stay on task, and a checker to ask questions verifying that the group agrees with the recorded information. (Assign roles when the group work starts.)

4. Tell the students that after the group has agreed on five commonalities and one unique attribute per person, they are to design a group crest that pictures those ideas. The body of the crest will contain the common attributes; three "corners" will be used to show the unique attributes. Stress that smiley faces and stick figures are just fine! Suggest that they find ways to divide up the work of actually producing the crest.

5. Tell the students that each group also needs a motto: a short, snappy saying that they believe summarizes the most outstanding commonality of the group. Model the final product with an example that represents yourself and two other people. Students will have fun with the model if the two other people are teachers they know.

6. Tell the students that they will have five minutes to brainstorm their lists and twenty minutes to produce their crests.

7. Ask the students to describe what they will be doing. Call on students at random to summarize the instructions.

8. Assign groups and working spaces for each group. Ask the students to get together quickly and quietly. When all students have finished moving, assign roles. You may want to say something like, "Whoever is wearing the most white today is your recorder. The person to the recorder's right is the conductor. The third person is the checker."

9. Help the students keep track of time. If you see that the time limits are too short, ask groups if they need more time. Ask them how much more time they realistically need.

10. When all of the crests are finished, ask each group to present its crest to the rest of the class. Ask the students if they want you to call on groups or if they want groups to volunteer. Encourage and model good listening during the presentations. After all of the crests have been presented, ask groups to tape their crests up on the walls in the room. Ask teammates to shake hands and thank each other for the successful completion of their task.

Stopping to Think

Ask groups to self-evaluate by answering the following questions: What were our best actions today (as a group)? What were our best thoughts? What skills would we like to strengthen the next time we work together? Do we need any help? Who do we need help from?

Ask each individual to self-evaluate by answering these questions in a personal journal: Which of my actions were most helpful to the group? Which of my thoughts were most helpful? What personal skills do I want to strengthen? How strong is my visual/spatial intelligence? How can I strengthen it? Do I need any help? Who can help me?

IRI/Skylight Training and Publishing, Inc.

Activity #3

Advanced Trust Builder

Getting on the Road

Once a basic level of trust is securely established, students will be able to form closer bonds. The more students feel that everyone is in this together, the more open they will be with self-evaluation. Students often say that the hardest part of being a member of a quality classroom is self-evaluation. I believe students say this because they feel that self-evaluation could open the doors to criticism and blaming, and they want to know that they are in a trusting environment before risking honest self-evaluation. Some students will find themselves a long way from their comfort zones before they finish this activity. It can be a lot of fun, and it can be a very good way to end an early week in the school year. It is done in groups of three. I suggest you use the same groups who designed the crests in the intermediate trust-building activity. Working with familiar people increases the comfort level. The teacher needs markers and chart paper.

Tell the students you want to find out what they know about a given topic. For example, because my students study water chemistry early in the year, I tell them, "I want to learn what you know about uses of water." Students have an opportunity to brainstorm lists of ideas to find out how much knowledge is available in a group, to act out their ideas, and to develop guidelines for future brainstorming sessions. I use the brainstorming guidelines to emphasize the importance of responsible behavior (more on this in chapter 2).

Cruising the Road

1. Instruct the class that each group will brainstorm as many uses of water as they can think of in three minutes. Let them know that each group will be asked to use its list in a certain way. Teachers from other disciplines may have their students brainstorm different topics. Asking students to act out some of the ideas they generate strengthens the activity. When choos-

ing topics, teachers may want to consider the possibilities for acting out ideas related to them.

In this activity, students use their **bodily/kinesthetic** intelligence to "act out" or pantomime an idea. They use their **interpersonal/social** intelligence to do small group work.

2. Ask the students to suggest rules for the brainstorm. Record their rules on chart paper so that the class can refer to them in the future. Some recommendations are (1) look for original ideas, (2) energize each other, (3) accept others' ideas, (4) rotate speakers, and (5) have numerous ideas. Encourage the students to "play" with the ideas.

3. Ask the class to describe the task (thus far). Call on students at random to summarize the instructions.

4. Assign the students to groups and have them gather quickly and quietly. When all students are settled, start the brainstorm. Help them keep track of time—you may want to give a one-minute warning before you announce that time is up.

5. Tell the students, "Now your group is going to act out three of your uses of water. As a group, decide what actions you are going to use to show those water uses to the rest of the class. You do not need to act out every use, just three of them. You will have five minutes to decide what uses your group wants to act out, to choose what actions you will use, and to practice those actions." Model the task. You may want to tell the students that they need to pick water uses that you did not act out.

6. Ask the students to describe the rest of the task. Call on students to summarize the instructions. Ask the students how they want you to signal that time is up for this phase of the activity. Having a predetermined signal is important—the room may become quite noisy.

7. When groups have completed this phase of the activity, ask them to demonstrate their actions for the rest of the class. Ask the other groups what is being acted out. Keep track of all of the different ideas that groups present.

8. Ask members of groups to shake hands and thank each other.

IRI/Skylight Training and Publishing, Inc.

Stopping to Think

Ask the students to self-evaluate by responding to the following questions in their journals: What were my best actions and thoughts today? What were my feelings about the acting-out task? What did I learn about learning by doing? How comfortable did I feel using my bodily/kinesthetic intelligence? What was my best teamwork today? What teamwork do I want to strengthen next time? Do I need help? Who do I see helping me?

Rules of the Road

Three Listening Exercises

Activity #1

Basic Listening Exercise

Getting on the Road

Listening is a very empowering activity. When someone listens to me and really focuses on what I am saying, I feel respected, trusted, accepted, and liked. I believe that students can become good listeners if they are given some guidance in listening skills and opportunities to practice those skills. I do this activity right after an initial trust builder to introduce the concept of responsible behavior and to develop some guidelines for responsible behavior in the classroom. I tell the students, "I have only one rule in this classroom. We will all use responsible behavior at all times. Responsible behavior helps a person get what he or she wants without hurting (or interfering with) anyone else." Once the students have that definition, I tell them that together we will develop a list of behaviors that fit the definition. I have the students select their own partners for this activity, and then we have an informal partner classroom meeting about establishing the rules. The teacher will need markers and chart paper for this activity.

Cruising the Road

In this activity, students use their **logical/ mathematical** intelligence to generalize from a list of specific examples. They use their **interpersonal/ social** intelligence to work with partners.

1. Introduce the concept of responsible behavior. Then tell the students that the activity will be done as a think/pair/share. Early in the year I always go over these instructions with the students: "Silently and individually think of your own answer(s) to the question. You may want to write them down. Discuss your answers quietly with a partner. Then, tell the class one of your answers. If possible, pick an answer that has not yet been given." I cue the students with the words "think" and "pair" to begin those two parts of the process. The students will need to decide how the sharing will be done before proceeding. So, I usually ask the following questions: How do you want to share? Do you want pairs to volunteer, or do you want me to call on teams?

2. Ask the students to pick their partners and move their desks together quickly and quietly. Wait for the students to complete their moves before continuing.

3. Ask the students, "What do people do and say when their behavior is responsible? Think of at least three answers. You will have thirty seconds to think of your answers." Repeat the question. Then say, "Think."

4. Watch the time carefully. After thirty seconds, say, "Pair. You have two minutes."

5. Watch the time carefully. After two minutes, signal for silence. I like to call every pair in the room at random. Record the answers on chart paper so you can save them.

6. When every pair has had an opportunity to answer, ask the class if they can find common threads to connect the answers. Then ask if the list can be used to develop a few positive classroom rules.

7. At this point, I do another think/pair/share question. This time the question is, "What is one positive classroom rule that you see in this list of questions?"

8. The following rules were commonly suggested from the list of questions:

   a. Be in class ready to start on time.

   b. Listen to whoever "has the floor."

   c. Focus on the topic being discussed.

   d. Use "put-ups" only—no putdowns in the classroom.

   e. Put your own things in their own place and let others do the same.

9. Help the students use a positive approach and focus on specific behaviors when wording the rules. Record the rules on the back of the chart paper you used to list responsible behaviors. When the list contains five or six rules, ask the students if they agree on the rules. Have the students sign the list. This action gives them ownership of the rules.

Stopping to Think

Have the students evaluate themselves in their journals by answering the following questions: What did I learn about responsible behavior today? What is my best responsible behavior? What irresponsible behavior do I use the most? How can I reduce my use of that behavior? How well do I use my logical/mathematical intelligence to generalize? How can I strengthen this intelligence? Do I need any help? Who do I see helping me?

Have the class agree on an action signal that will be used to remind anyone and everyone in the classroom to be a "good listener." Practice using the signal.

Activity #2

Intermediate Listening Exercise

Getting on the Road

It is empowering to have someone listen to you, but it is even more empowering to have a listener who agrees with your ideas. This activity is a structure for agreement and is done in randomly assigned groups of three. I do this activity very early in the year to help the students learn that being able to work pleasantly and politely with a wide variety of people is an important real-life skill. Each group will need a sheet of chart paper and some colored markers.

I ask the students if they remember any advertising slogans that use the word *quality*. We usually come up with "quality is job one," "the quality goes in before the name goes on," "when quality counts," and several others. I ask the students what the word *quality* really means; what it looks like; and what people do, think, and feel when they experience quality. I write the questions on the board or on chart paper as I go.

Cruising the Road

1. Tell the students that their job will be to define *quality* in as many ways as they can.

2. Tell them that each group will have a speaker, a listener, and a recorder. The roles will rotate with each new idea. The speaker will say, "I think that quality is (or looks like, or feels like). . . ." The listener will listen to the speaker and then answer, "I like that idea because. . . ." The recorder will write down the idea and the "I like." For the second idea, roles rotate one person to the right. The first speaker is now the recorder, the first listener is now the speaker, and the first recorder is now the listener.

3. Tell students that the roles will rotate around the group three times so that everyone has a chance to state three ideas, tell why they like three ideas, and write down three ideas and likes.

IRI/Skylight Training and Publishing, Inc.

4. Give an example, such as, "Quality is the best job that I can do at this time in my life." "I like that idea because it says that people develop and grow and may not have the skills to do perfect work right now!"

5. Ask the students to describe what they will be doing. Call on students at random to review the instructions.

In this activity, students use their **verbal/ linguistic** intelligence to develop a definition. They use their **interpersonal/social** intelligence to act as members of small groups.

6. Assign the students to groups and assign the roles randomly; for example, designate the oldest person in the group as the first speaker. The person to the speaker's right will be the first listener, and the third person will be the recorder. Ask the recorder to use a piece of chart paper and some colored markers to make the list of ideas and likes.

7. Tell the groups that they have ten minutes to do the job. Keep track of the time. If groups say that they need more time, ask them how much more time they will realistically need to finish the job.

8. When groups have finished, make a master list of ideas.

9. Tell the students about Dr. William Glasser and his belief that quality can only be achieved in a trusting, supportive place (like the classroom). Let them know that quality is always useful and that it is always the best that a person or group can do. Quality always feels good without being destructive (it is responsible). Quality is tested and improved by self-evaluation. Ask the students how closely they agree with Dr. Glasser. (I find that the students' ideas are very close to Dr. Glasser's.)

10. Now that the groups have defined *quality,* make up a quality cheer that you are willing to demonstrate to the rest of the class. Give them an example: "Quality, quality, that's our game! We're so proud of our work that we sign our name!" The sillier your example is, the more creative their cheers will be.

11. Ask groups if they want to volunteer to give their cheers, or if they want you to call on groups at random.

Stopping to Think

In their journals, have the students answer the following questions: What did I learn about quality today? What work do I do that is always quality? How can I improve the quality of my work? Do I need help? Who do I see helping me? How well did I use my verbal/linguistic intelligence today? How can I strengthen it? Ask each student to include a sketch of someone or something that he or she perceives as being quality.

Activity #3

Advanced Listening Exercise

Getting on the Road

I believe that sometimes it is important for the students to have a controlled need-frustrating experience followed quickly by a need-satisfying experience. Telling a story to someone who is focused on him- or herself can lead to a feeling of powerlessness or rejection on the part of the speaker. This activity can be very need unsatisfying at first, so I recommend that it be done after some level of trust exists in the classroom. It is also very important to do the positive activity as soon as the negative activity has been processed. I want the students to leave the room on a "high" that results from having their needs met. Students will do this activity with a partner they have chosen.

Ask the students to think of a really good story about themselves—a positive experience. It could be a time when they had fun in school, did well athletically, received some special award or recognition, had fun with their families—just as long as it is a story they can tell some-one in about three minutes. Tell them to keep that story in mind while you give the instructions for the activity.

Cruising the Road

In this activity, students use their **verbal/ linguistic** intelligence to tell a story, their **intrapersonal/ introspective** intelligence to analyze their own feelings, and their **interpersonal/social** intelligence to work with a partner.

1. Tell the students to pick a partner and move close to him or her. Tell them that they will receive further instructions as soon as they have found partners.

2. When the students have all found partners, tell them to find out which partner is older. Tell them that the older partner is the storyteller, whose job it is to tell his or her story to the listener. The listener's job is to interrupt the storyteller by saying, "That's like the time when I. . . ." In other words, the listener switches the focus to herself or himself. The story-teller is to do his or her best to finish the original story. The listener is to do his or her best to switch to a different story. Tell the students a story that models the process. For example, I once began telling an acquaintance about the surprise family portrait we had taken for my mother-in-law's eightieth birth-day, only to have the person interrupt by saying, "Well, my mother-in-law is seventy-five and she and I have never gotten along. She always felt that her son was too good for me. There was the time when. . . ." The focus was reversed, and she was off and running.

3. Ask the students what they are to do. Call on students to summarize the process.

4. Begin the storytelling round. Be a careful timekeeper. The storytellers may show signs of anger or frustration before time is officially up. You may end the round early if you believe it would be prudent.

5. Ask the students to write a quick journal entry beginning like the following: "When I was interrupted (or when I interrupted my partner), I felt . . . ; I thought . . . ; I did. . . ."

6. Ask the students to share answers with the rest of the class. Asking for volunteers is a good idea here. Some students may not feel comfortable talking about their feelings in front of the class. Record the feelings, thoughts, and actions on the black-board or on chart paper.

7. Now tell the students that you want to change the activity. The storyteller has the same job. Tell the story he or she tried to tell before. The listener is to focus on the story and ask ques-tions that encourage the storyteller to clarify or expand the story.

8. Ask the students to summarize the new instructions and begin the new round.

9. Ask the students to write a new journal entry describing their feelings, thoughts, and actions as they were listened to or as they listened. Ask the students to share these ideas with the rest of the class. Record their new ideas on the back of the first list.

10. Ask the students which list shows the results of responsible behavior. Ask the students to sign the list to show their agreement with responsible behavior.

Stopping to Think

Ask partners to co-verify the listening behaviors that were used during the second round of storytelling. What behaviors were most effective? What listening behaviors do they think they use well? What skills would they like to strengthen? Do they see themselves helping each other practice listening skills? How comfortable were they in using their intrapersonal intelligence to evaluate their partners' feelings? How well did they use their verbal intelligence (in storytelling or questioning)? How well did they use their social intelligence? Ask them to complete this analogy: "Good listening is like a gentle rainfall because. . . ."

• Part II •

Teaching Control Theory to Students

Shifting Gears

Using Control Theory

An Interactive Introduction to Control Theory

Getting on the Road

You may use this tool very early in the year. I use it the second or third day of school to introduce control theory vocabulary and to encourage the students to start thinking about their needs and about total behavior. During the first part of the activity I have the opportunity to watch the social dynamics of the class. This helps me identify students who are somewhat shy and those who are very social. I like to use this information to put together the groups later.

For this activity, each student will need a copy of the "People Search" form at the end of this chapter. Ask the students to think of five things they believe they really *need*. Tell them to jot down a list of their needs. Tell them they will be asked to share some of their needs with the rest of the class after you have done an activity focusing on needs and behaviors. The things may be objects, permissions, behaviors, feelings—whatever comes to mind.

Cruising the Road

In this activity, students use their **bodily/kinesthetic** intelligence as they move from person to person. They use their **interpersonal/ social** intelligence to get signatures during the people search and their **verbal/ linguistic** intelligence during discussion.

1. Hand out the "People Search" form.

2. Tell the students the rules:

   a. A classmate is to sign for each of the items on the people search.

   b. A *different* classmate is to sign each item, so they will have a total of nine *different* signatures.

   c. The classmate will tell why he or she is able to sign (give information or an answer for the item on the "People Search" form).

3. Inform the students that the requirement for nine *different* signatures means they will be getting out of their desks and moving around the room. Ask for ideas about how to keep the room fairly quiet and how they want you to signal for them to stop talking.

4. Ask the students (rhetorically): "What is a good way to get what you want from someone else? How about giving that person something that he or she wants? A good way to get a signature from someone is to offer to give that person a signature. Make good eye contact with that person. Call him or her by name. Create a helping environment. For example, I may walk up to Reita and say, 'Hi, Reita. I can sign number seven for you. I'll have fun in school as soon as everyone else has a chance to start doing this activity. Do you want me to sign your "People Search" form?' My offering to give a signature may help me get a signature."

5. Ask the students what they will be doing. Call on students at random to summarize the instructions.

6. Set a time limit (I recommend ten minutes for this people search) and start the activity.

7. Be a careful timekeeper. I find it helpful to model the requested behavior by circulating among students to get my copy of the "People Search" form signed. After ten minutes, signal for silence and ask the students to return to their seats.

8. A full discussion of this people search takes me at least the rest of the class period. I will carry the discussion over to the beginning of the next class period if I run out of time on the first day. To start the discussion, ask students to go back to their list of needs that they were asked to write down before we started the people search. Ask each student to come to the board and write down one of their needs. Ask them to try to find a need that is different from anyone else's. I like to call groups of five or six students up to the board at the same time to speed up the process and to help students avoid the "spotlight."

9. Once every student has had an opportunity to contribute one need to the list, use this opportunity to discuss Dr. Glasser's theory of being born with five basic, genetic needs that determine our behaviors: belonging, power, survival, fun, and freedom. I write the needs on a sheet of chart paper as I name them. Then I ask the students which of the needs we have listed on the board could be a specific *want* that helps us get more belonging. I encourage students to look over the list and find four or five belonging wants. As they name the wants, I record them with the need on the chart paper. If a want seems to fit with more than one need, I write it in a special color. The format for the needs chart is given below (with some wants examples filled in).

OUR FIVE BASIC NEEDS

Belonging	friends, athletic teams, family, band
Power	name in school paper, computer proficiency, good grades, friends
Survival	money, pizza, home, physical safety
Fun	movies, MTV, friends, sports
Freedom	car, stay out late, weekends

10. I ask the students to look at their needs, which we are now calling wants, and explain that Dr. Glasser refers to these wants as "pictures" that each of us has in our "quality world." He says that when we choose a picture or a want, we choose it to satisfy one or more of the basic needs. I ask the students to look at the wants in our chart that meet more than one need. Then I tell them to ask themselves how important that want is to them. The more need-satisfying a picture is, the stronger it is.

11. Finally, ask the students to look over the items on the people search again. Mention words used that refer to behaviors: brainstorming, laughing, crying, running, biking, swimming, living, being healthy. Explain that Dr. Glasser states that all we can do to meet our needs is behave, and our behavior has four components: acting, thinking, feeling, and physiology. We choose our behaviors. No one "makes" us do anything. We act; we do not *react*. The one component of behavior that we are always aware of is *feeling*. The components that we can most easily control are *thinking* and *acting*. Ask the students to think about the implications of changing their feelings. Ask them if they believe people can change their feelings by changing their actions or thoughts. Can *doing* something positive and *thinking* something positive help you *feel* better?

Stopping to Think

Ask the students to complete in their journal the following statements: "Doing the people search helped me meet my need for belonging by. . . . It helped me meet my need for *power, freedom,* and *fun* by. . . . During the people search, I did . . . ; thought . . . ; and felt. . . . I felt comfortable (or uncomfortable) using my social intelligence because. . . . "

Suggest that school can become an important part of their quality worlds if they see that school is a need-satisfying place. Ask each student to write down the titles of two "quality world" songs (my favorites are "We Shall Overcome" and "Ode to Joy").

PEOPLE SEARCH

Give a signature, get a signature. Get a different signature for each of the following.

Find someone who...

belongs to at least one club or team	can brainstorm at least three reasons for an electrical power failure
has been healthy for the past month	prefers to save money rather than spend it
can name Simba's evil uncle in *The Lion King*	says (s)he laughs or cries easily
can predict the next time (s)he will have fun in school	enjoys running, biking, swimming, or skateboarding
"lives for the moment"	uses the Internet at home

Activity #2

Examining the Five Basic Needs

Getting on the Road

I do this activity a few days after the control theory people search to review the five basic needs and to develop some more pictures of ways in which students meet those needs. I like to help students discover that there are many ways to meet each need, and I also like knowing that when I talk about one of the needs they understand what I am saying. I like knowing, in other words, that the students and I are on the same wavelength. This activity also helps students see that they can meet a need without getting a specific want. They can substitute a different want and still meet the need.

I begin by telling students that we are going to review what we have learned about the five basic needs. I call on a randomly selected student to name one of the needs, and begin a needs list on the blackboard. I continue calling on randomly selected students until all five of the needs are listed. (The first year that I taught control theory to students, I felt surprised at the number of guesses we took before all five of the needs had been named. Then I asked myself why I felt so surprised. I could not realistically expect students to memorize the names of the needs on the basis of a single introductory activity.) Next, I look at the list of needs and burst into song:

> (sung to the tune of "Battle Hymn of the Republic")
>
> Freedom, fun, belonging, power—
>
> Freedom, fun, belonging, power—
>
> Freedom, fun, belonging, power—
>
> and survival are our basic needs.

My singing is usually greeted with lots of laughter. After the laughing subsides, I tell students that they will be working in small groups to write the rest of the song about the five basic needs.

Cruising the Road

In this activity, students use their **musical/ rhythmic** intelligence to write and perform one verse of a song. They use their **visual/ spatial** intelligence to illustrate their song verse, and their **interpersonal/ social** intelligence to work in small groups.

1. Tell the students that each group will write, illustrate, and perform one verse of a "basic needs" song using the "Mine Eyes Have Seen the Glory" rhythm and rhyme scheme. Each verse will focus on one of the basic needs. Give the groups their needs assignments when you have finished explaining the rest of the instructions.

2. Each verse will include the name of a need, a brief explanation of the need, and at least three examples of ways in which people meet the need.

3. Each group will make a graphic that illustrates its song verse. The graphic will include a symbol representing the need and illustrations of the ways people meet the need.

4. Each group will need a composer to keep the group on task, a designer to coordinate the production of the graphic, a lyricist to keep notes about the song lyric and ways to satisfy the need, a grip to get production materials, and some production assistants to help get the graphic done.

5. Summarize the instructions: Each group will write a "battle hymn" verse about its assigned need. The verse will include a brief definition of the need and at least three examples of ways to satisfy the need. The group will also produce a graphic that illustrates the need and ways to satisfy it. The groups will each perform their verses for the class while displaying the graphics. The graphics will then be used to decorate the room.

6. Be sure the students understand the instructions. Call on randomly selected students to summarize or paraphrase the instructions.

7. Assign the students to their groups. I use only five groups for this activity. Large groups seem to help students feel more comfortable about doing a song. Before I do this activity, I also find out who the band, choir, and drama people are, and I build the groups around them. The presence of that performance person in the group seems to help others when the time to perform comes. My singing introduction of the activity models for the students that it is all right to take a risk and perform. No one will laugh at another person's performance in this class.

8. Assign a need to each group: group 1 is survival, group 2 is belonging, group 3 is power, group 4 is freedom, and group 5 is fun.

9. Give groups twenty minutes to write the song verse and do the graphic. After twenty minutes, ask groups if they are finished. If they are not, ask how much more time they reasonably and realistically need. Give them time to finish.

10. When all of the groups have finished, ask the class to come back together. Ask students if they want to volunteer to perform or if they want you to call on groups at random. Have the lyrics for the chorus on the board or the overhead projector. Start with the whole class singing the chorus; then have each group perform its verse. Finish with the whole class chorus once again. Lead the class in a round of applause. Ask each group to hang its graphic on the wall. You may want to cluster the graphics together to produce a "needs graffiti wall."

Stopping to Think

Tell students that while they were doing this activity, they were using two intelligences that are frequently overlooked in the classroom: musical/rhythmic and visual/spatial. Ask each individual to write a journal entry describing his or her comfort level about being asked to sing in class and a time when he or she remembers feeling comfortable about singing in class. Ask: "Is your comfort level better, about the same, or worse than it was then? How can you practice using this intelligence?"

Ask each individual to continue by answering these questions: Which need do you believe may be your strongest? Which need do you think you satisfy the least often? Include support for your answers to these questions.

Activity #3

Examining Internal Motivation for Behavior

Getting on the Road

As long as students continue to interpret their actions using stimulus-response theory, it is easy for them to see themselves as victims of the schemes of others, as puppets who are manipulated by others, or as innocents who blame others for everything that goes wrong. When students begin to understand that their actions are internally motivated and are chosen to help them get something they want—something that is a need-satisfying picture—they take ownership of their behavior and its consequences. They begin to understand that they can learn new behaviors that may help them take more effective control of their lives. This activity is done in small groups that are assigned randomly. Each student needs a copy of the "Do You Always . . ." and "Making Sense of Your Action" sheets found at the end of this chapter.

I like to introduce this activity by discussing a situation that the students and I have in common. For example, I may ask them, "Do you always move quickly to the nearest exit when you hear the fire alarm go off?" Most students will answer, "Yes!" I ask them why they behave this way, and they answer, "That's how we have been taught to react." (Their answer may use different words, but I can get the word *react* or *respond* in an answer if I just dig around a little.) My next question is, "Do you *react* to the alarm or do you get a picture that satisfies a need by choosing that behavior? Does the alarm *make* you hurry to an exit or is that a behavior you choose? Might there be other behaviors you would use sometimes? Might you delay leaving the building because there is another picture that you want? Please just think about your answer for now."

Cruising the Road

In this activity, students use their **logical/mathematical** intelligence to analyze a behavior. They use their **interpersonal/social** intelligence to act as members of small groups.

---

1. Hand out copies of the two sheets. Ask the students to read and answer the questions silently and individually.

2. Tell the students that, as a member of a small group, they will be asked to examine their answers to one of the questions. First the group will discuss if and when they do something other than the action referred to in the question (i.e., Do they always hit their lockers when they are jammed?). The group's second job is to make sense of the actions they take by looking at their "Making Sense of Your Actions" worksheet. Each group will have a recorder to write down the consensus answers, a checker to ask questions that ensure all group members understand and agree with the answers to the "Making Sense" questions, a reporter to read the group's answer to the rest of the class, a conductor to watch the time and encourage the group to stay on task, and a linguist to help the group state its answer in control theory language.

3. Go over an example from the "Making Sense" worksheet. I usually follow up my initial question by asking myself in front of the class, "What do I think when I hear the fire alarm go off? I think there may be a fire. What do I want? I want to be safe and unhurt by the fire. What do I want when I head for the nearest exit? I want to get away from the possible fire as fast as I can. What need am I meeting? The need for survival. But do I always go to the nearest exit immediately? No. Sometimes I check restrooms to be sure that they are empty or hold doors to help others get downstairs quickly. Helping others get out of harm's way gives me *freedom* from worry about leaving them trapped in a burning building and *power* over myself (I didn't panic!)."

4. Ask the students what their task is. Call on students at random to summarize the instructions.

5. Tell the students that groups will have ten minutes to get together and come up with answers to the "Making Sense" worksheet. Tell them that the ten minutes includes time for the reporter to practice delivering the answer so that the rest of the class can hear and understand it.

6. Assign groups and role assignments. When the groups have formed, assign the roles randomly, such as having the member of the group who lives closest to school take the role of reporter. Then, the person to the recorder's right can be the recorder, next can be the checker, then the conductor, and finally the

linguist. Assign one specific "Do You Always" question to each group. Be sure that each group knows which question it is working with.

7. Be a careful timekeeper. Let groups know when they have two minutes left to finish the activity. My students also appreciate a thirty-second warning.

8. Ask groups if they want to volunteer to give their "Making Sense" answers or if they want you to call on groups at random.

9. Model good listening as groups give their answers.

Stopping to Think

Ask each group to design a two-panel graphic. The first panel will contain stimulus-response words surrounded by the international "banned" signal. The second panel will contain corresponding control theory vocabulary. Show students an example:

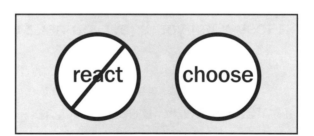

Ask each group to brainstorm five examples for each category. Give groups time to generate their ideas. Have two circles on a sheet of chart paper taped to the front board of the room. Ask each group to send its linguist to the board to write a word in each circle. Post the finished product in a place where the students can refer to it often. At the end of any group activity, I like to ask the students to shake hands with the members of their groups and thank them for the work they did together. Ask the students to answer these questions: How comfortable were you when you used your logical/ mathematical intelligence to analyze the behavior? How can you strengthen this intelligence?

DO YOU ALWAYS . . .

Hit your locker when it is jammed?

Stop for the crossing gates at the railroad tracks?

Answer the telephone when you are home alone?

Get up as soon as you hear your alarm clock?

Study for a test when you know you have one?

Put materials away (clean up) when a teacher asks you to?

WHO CONTROLS YOUR BEHAVIOR?

DO YOU ACT OR REACT?

MAKING SENSE OF YOUR ACTIONS

What do you want when your locker is jammed?	What do you want to happen when you hit your locker? What need will you meet if you get what you want? What else might you do? What would that get you?
What does it mean when the railroad crossing gates go down? What are you thinking when you see that happen?	What do you want to get by stopping? What need are you meeting? What else might you do? What would that get you?
What might it mean when the telephone rings?	What do you get when you answer the phone? What need might you be meeting? What else might you do? When might you do it? What would that get you?
What does it mean when your alarm goes off?	What will you get if you get up? How important is it to have that? What need are you meeting by getting up? What else might you do? What might that get you?
What do you want to have happen when you take a test?	Will studying help you get what you want? What need will that meet? What else could you do? What would that get you?
What does "time to clean up" usually mean?	What will you get if you "clean up" when the teacher asks you to? What need will that meet? What else could you do? When might you do something else? What will you get?

Activity #4

A Closer Look at Who Controls Behavior

Getting on the Road

Many of my students arrive in my classroom believing that they do *not* choose or control their own behaviors. They perceive their lives as being controlled by others. They are willing or unwilling victims of the desires of their peers, families, teachers—the list could go on and on. I want to give them the opportunity to practice a new perception: they choose and control their own behaviors. This activity is done individually. Each student needs a copy of "Choose—or Blame and Excuse?" found at the end of this chapter.

As soon as the bell rings to begin class, greet the students and ask them who or what *made* them get to class on time? Tell them you want them to think about an answer because you will be asking some of them to share their answers with the rest of the class. After the students have thought about their answers for a few seconds, call on a number of students for their answers. Record the answers on the blackboard. When you have collected five or six different answers, ask the students to look at the answers. Then ask the following questions: Did anyone or anything *make* you get here on time or did you *want* to get here on time? Did you choose to act in a way that would get you to class on time because those actions would get you something else that you want? What do you get that you want when you choose on-time behaviors?

I tell the students to think about an answer they can share with the rest of the class. Then, I share one of mine: "When I get to class on time, I see myself as behaving responsibly and professionally—I'm here on time to lead a class I contracted to teach. I see myself as someone who keeps her word. I also see myself as someone who wants to help others (you, the students). Finally, I like you and I want to be here on time because I feel happy when I do the 'right' thing for people I like." After the students have had a few seconds to think of answers, call on them again. Record their answers on the board. Then ask, "Does anyone ever really *make* you do anything? Or do you choose your behaviors to get 'quality world' pictures that you want? Dr. Glasser says that we can control our own behaviors and we can influence others if we are in their quality worlds, but we do not *make* anyone else do anything. We choose behaviors that help us meet our needs."

Cruising the Road

In this activity, students use their **intrapersonal/ introspective** intelligence to examine the internal motivation for behavior. They use their **interpersonal/social** intelligence during small group discussions.

1. Hand out "Choose—or Blame and Excuse?" sheets.

2. Go over the instructions and the example with the students. Point out the *need* that is implied by the rewritten statement. Emphasize the idea that we choose behaviors that are need-satisfying. We choose our wants—our quality world pictures—because they are need-satisfying pictures.

3. Ask students to identify the need they are meeting by choosing the behavior in the rewritten statement. Ask them to analyze the total behavior—what are they doing, thinking, and feeling, and what is the body saying as they engage the behavior?

4. Give the students some quiet, individual time to start doing the activity during class. I like to tell the students, "To be ready for class tomorrow, please complete your work for at least five of the statements. You will be discussing and analyzing your answers in small groups tomorrow."

5. Assign the small groups at the beginning of the next class period. Ask the students to share their work with members of their groups, focusing on the need that is being met and the total behavior that is being used to meet that need. Ask, "What can you do to give everyone in your group an equal chance to speak?" Set a time limit for the discussion.

6. Ask the students to summarize the instructions. Have groups form quickly and quietly and begin discussing the activity.

7. As you monitor the groups, listen for vocabulary that indicates discussion of needs and of total behaviors.

8. Ask the members of the groups to shake hands and thank each other at the end of the discussion time.

Stopping to Think

Ask the students to write thoughtful answers in their journals to the following questions: What needs do I meet when I blame others for my behavior? What needs do I meet when I recognize my control over my own behavior? Do I want to see myself as a victim or as someone who is in control? How can I see myself the way I want to? How comfortable am I when I use my intrapersonal intelligence to examine my internal motivation for behaviors? How can I increase my comfort level? A song that helps me remember I am in control is. . . . When I picture myself in control, I see . . . (sketch it or write it in words).

CHOOSE—OR BLAME AND EXCUSE?

Rewrite each of these "made me" statements as an "I choose" statement. Identify the need(s) that are met by choosing the behaviors and the acting, thinking, feeling, and physiological components of the behaviors.

Example

Statement	Rewrite	Need(s)	Components
He made me **so** happy!	I was so happy when I was with him that I felt like dancing!	Belonging, fun	Acting: dancing, laughing Thinking: I want to dance! I want this to go on and on! Feeling: happy Physiology: alert, "warm inside"

"Made Me" Statements

1. The teacher made me do homework instead of going to the big game.

2. Mom made me mad when she said that I was grounded.

3. My boss made me happy when he told me that I was getting a raise.

4. My friends made me feel good when they asked me to go out with them.

5. This cold made me fall asleep so I couldn't finish my assignment.

6. That teacher made me late for class. She said I couldn't run in the halls.

7. Susie made me talk to her (while her teacher was talking).

8. That teacher made me look stupid by calling on me when he knew I didn't know the answer.

Who's Driving? You or Me?

Gaining Control

Activity #1

Perceptions about Control

Getting on the Road

Many students feel their wheels slipping and spinning as they use time and energy worrying over things they can't control. They can experience some freedom from frustration if they take the time to identify what they can control, what they can influence, and what they cannot control. Here are two activities to be done individually. One helps students identify control in their personal lives; the other focuses their attention on control in school. Each student needs a copy of each "Perceiving Control from the 'Right Angle'" worksheet found at the end of this chapter.

I like to introduce this activity with a personal anecdote. I'll say something like, "I really felt like my wheels were spinning this morning. The temperature in the room felt like one hundred degrees when I opened the door. Did I see red! I started complaining to anyone who was around about how cheap this school is—can't they even run the air conditioning long enough to cool off the room before classes start? Don't they know that we don't have windows? I'll bet things would be different if this were an administrative office instead of a classroom. Then, all of a sudden, I heard myself and I thought: Wait a minute! Can I control whether or not the AC was turned on early today? No! Am I wasting my time complaining and blaming? You bet! What *can* I control that might improve the situation? Once I changed the direction of my thinking, I started feeling less frustrated and found things to do—like propping open the doors to let in the cooler hall air." Then I ask the students, "Do you ever feel like your wheels have lost their traction? Could it be that you're doing what I was doing—fuming over things that you can't control? What do you think?"

Cruising the Road

In this activity, students use their **intrapersonal/ introspective** intelligence to examine what they can control in school and outside of school. They use their **verbal/linguistic** intelligence to express their ideas, and their **bodily/kinesthetic** intelligence to invent "in-control" and "out-of-control" signals.

1. Hand out copies of the "Perceiving Control" worksheet that has the statement, "In my own life, I can control. . . ."

2. Help the students begin by telling them they should put each item in front of one of the arrows.

3. Ask them, "Are there things that you cannot control but you can influence? Where would you like to place those items?"

4. Stress the idea that you are asking them to do this exercise for their own understanding. Ask them if they will feel more powerful or less powerful if they spend more time on what they can control and less time on what they cannot control. Will they have more freedom from frustration that way? Will they feel in more effective control? Inform the students that this activity is a quick way to help them practice asking themselves this question: Can I control that?

5. Hand out the other "Perceiving Control" worksheet (it has the statement, "When I am in school . . .") on another day. Remind the students of your reasons for asking them to do this kind of activity. Ask them, "Will school be a more pleasant place if we all stop spinning our wheels over things that we cannot control? Will we have more success if we focus on the things that we can control?"

6. Suggest that the students file these worksheets someplace where they can add items to them from time to time.

Stopping to Think

Ask the students to invent a hand signal they can use to remind each other to focus on things they can control. Ask what they can do to signal to someone that his or her wheels are spinning. Ask what they can do to signal to someone that they are cruising! Ask for examples of other times when people use their bodily/kinesthetic intelligence (rather than words) to deliver a message. Ask the students if their comfort in using interpersonal intelligence is increasing. Ask how they can become stronger in using this intelligence. Have the class agree on a set of hand signals and practice using them.

PERCEIVING CONTROL FROM THE "RIGHT ANGLE"

Place each phrase in front of the arrow where it fits best.

- The weather
- Who my parents are
- Who my friends are
- Keeping my room cleaned up
- Feeling "in charge"
- Studying/Doing schoolwork
- My friends' feelings
- What I buy with my money
- Living by the rules
- When I go to sleep

- When I get up in the morning
- Where I live
- How much "junk food" I eat
- How much my parents "lecture"
- How often I ask for advice
- My actions
- My language
- Who I "hang out" with
- My thoughts
- Getting around
  (by car? bike? skateboard? walking?)

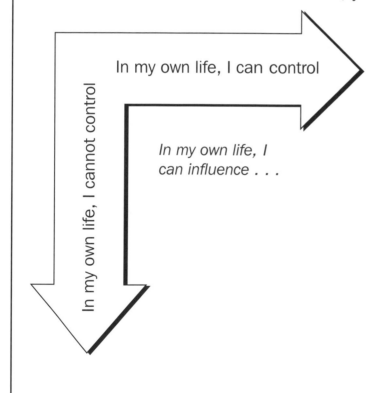

In my own life, I can control

In my own life, I cannot control

In my own life, I can influence . . .

What other things can I add to each category?

PERCEIVING CONTROL FROM THE "RIGHT ANGLE"

Place each phrase in front of the arrow where it fits best.

- The size of my classrooms
- The temperature of my classrooms
- The weight of my books
- How much my teachers lecture
- Asking for help when I need it
- Doing quality homework
- Hours spent working outside of school
- Being a quality learner
- Who my friends are
- Being in classes with my friends

- The size of the hallways
- How fast I walk to class
- "Hanging on to" my books
- How well I take notes
- How much homework my teachers assign
- Getting days off
- Which clubs/teams I join
- Remembering books/pencils/paper
- Staying awake
- Cooperating with my classmates and teachers

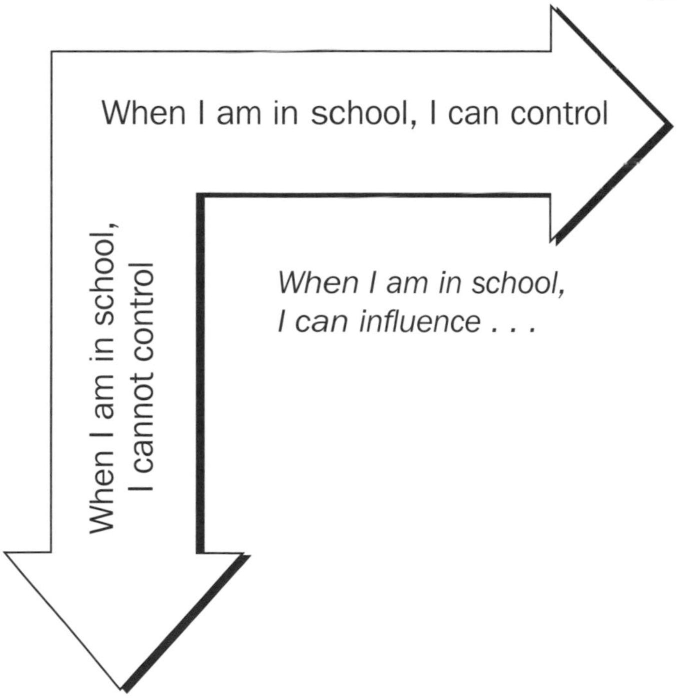

When I am in school, I can control

When I am in school, I cannot control

When I am in school, I can influence . . .

What other things can I add to each category?

Activity #2

Sorting out Responsibilities

Getting on the Road

When I was a very young teacher, I felt shock, disbelief, and then amusement one day when a student walked up to my desk and said, "You know, I have a B average in science, and it is your job to maintain it." At the time I did not know control theory, but my picture of reality was that the work students did determined their grades in a course. I said, "I will be happy to be the bookkeeper in this class. I will record the grades for the work that you do. If you do B work, the records will show that your grade is a B. He thought for a moment, then said, "OK. That sounds fair." As he walked away I thought how important it is for the students and teachers to know just what their job is in the classroom (and what their job is *not).* This activity focuses student attention on this issue. I like to use a Venn diagram to show that some responsibilities are shared, and to emphasize the idea that we really are all in this together. Each student will need a copy of "Yours, Mine, Ours—Whose Job Is It?," found at the end of this section.

Ask the students, "Have you ever thought about who's in charge of what job at home? Here's a little something that I devised to help you focus on who is responsible for doing what at home. Please use the next few moments to fill in the Venn diagram." This may be the first time you have given an assignment involving a Venn diagram. If so, review the rules for using Venn diagrams. I usually ask the students, "Do you know how to use this?" Several students in the class will answer, "Yes," and I ask them to list the rules for the rest of the class.

After the students have filled in their individual Venn diagrams, I ask them to compare their answers with a neighbor's answers (I may assign "neighbors"). Then I tell them that their next job will be to examine jobs in the classroom.

Cruising the Road

In this activity, students use their **visual/ spatial** intelligence to fill in a Venn diagram. They use their **interpersonal/ social** intelligence to work in small groups and their **verbal/ linguistic** intelligence to examine the list of responsibilities.

1. Hand out copies of the "Whose Job Is It in School?" worksheet. Tell the students that their job for the next class meeting is to decide where they want to place each item in the Venn diagram. Tell them that they will discuss their ideas in class—first in small groups, and then as a whole class.

2. At the beginning of the next class period, tell the students they will first discuss their ideas in small groups. Each group will need a recorder to fill out the group copy of the Venn diagram, a checker to ask members of the group to clarify their positions and check for agreement, and a reporter to speak for the group during the whole class discussion. Tell the students that they will have ten minutes for the small group discussion. At the end of that time, each group is to have a filled-in Venn diagram.

3. Ask the students to review the task. Call on the students at random to summarize the task.

4. Assign the groups. Ask the group's recorder to pick up a clean copy of the Venn diagram.

5. Help groups watch the time. Give a two-minute warning, a thirty-second warning, and a "time's up" signal.

6. Ask the reporters to identify themselves. Ask if they want to volunteer or if they want you to call on them randomly.

7. Lead the class discussion. Fill in a copy of the Venn diagram on large chart paper as the class reaches consensus on ideas. Be sure to ask groups to talk about ideas that were *not* listed on the original assignment sheet.

8. Post the completed large Venn diagram somewhere that the students can see it.

Stopping to Think

Discuss using the Venn diagram as a visual/spatial tool to make thinking visible. Ask the students to write their thoughts about the following in their journals: Now I understand that my jobs in this class include . . . (pick the two that you feel are the most important). The thing that I liked the most about this activity was. . . . The idea that I heard that surprised me the most is. . . . Then ask them to jot down some thoughts about what jobs are not theirs or yours. Tell them that you will ask them to share those thoughts with the rest of the class the next day. Coming back to those thoughts the next day helps reinforce the idea that someone outside of the immediate classroom circle does some jobs that affect the classroom circle. Someone else is in control of those jobs.

YOURS, MINE, OURS—WHOSE JOB IS IT?

Where does each of the following fit best in the Venn diagram?

- Making the house payments
- Shoveling the snow
- Cleaning my room
- Doing the laundry
- Paying the utility bills
- Cooking meals
- Feeding the pets
- Sorting materials for recycling
- Getting me up for school
- Paying the phone bill
- Cleaning the bathroom

- Mowing the lawn
- Paying for groceries/food
- Driving the family car responsibly
- Cleaning the kitchen
- Making car payments
- Washing the car
- Putting out the garbage
- Filling the car with gas
- Watching younger children
- Doing my homework

What else do you want to add?
Where do you want to place it?

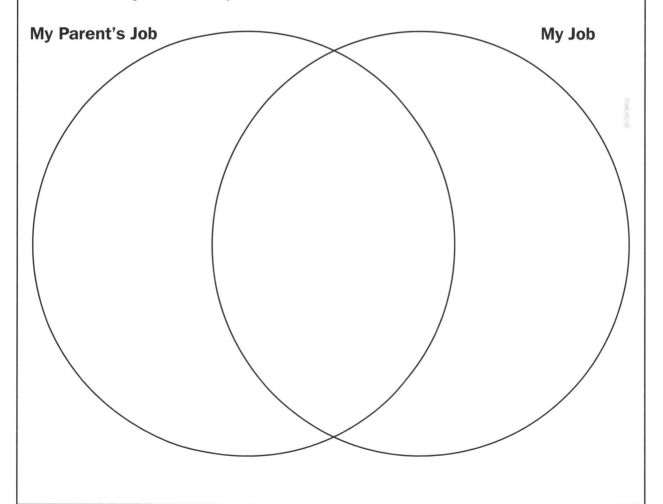

My Parent's Job   My Job

YOURS, MINE, OURS—WHOSE JOB IS IT IN SCHOOL?

Where does each of the following fit best in the Venn diagram?

- Taking attendance
- Evaluating my work
- Maintaining order in the classroom
- Showing respect to students in the class
- Remembering due dates
- Being prepared for class
- Providing me with pen or pencil and paper
- Keeping track of my grades
- Getting what I want responsibly

- Reporting attendance
- Being a course content "expert"
- Developing the course schedule
- Getting to class on time
- Explaining/teaching material
- Being sure I learn
- Tutoring
- Helping others
- Being sure I know what I missed when I am absent

What else do you want to add?
Where do you want to place it?

My Teacher's Job   **My Job**

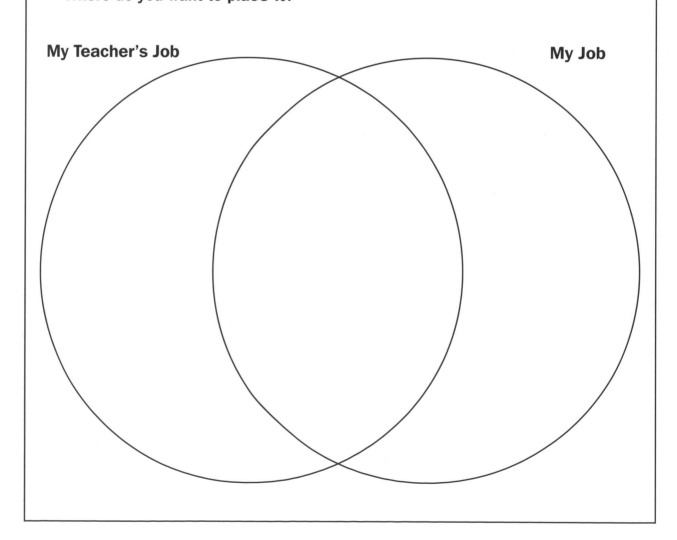

IRI/Skylight Training and Publishing, Inc.

Activity #3

Components of Total Behavior

Getting on the Road

When I first studied control theory, I frequently used my old definition of behavior—behavior meant acting. I needed time and practice to remember that there are four components of total behavior—acting, thinking, feeling, and physiology. Students seem to need the same time and practice that I did. I like to use base groups for this activity. The trust level that students establish in their base groups helps them to really "ham it up," and the more they do, the more fun we all have.

Do a think/pair/share with your students. Ask them, "When you were little, did your mother ever tell you to behave? What did she mean by that? Did she mean act your age, or be more quiet, or stop fighting with your little sister, or what?" Give students a few seconds to think of individual answers. Ask them to pick a partner and exchange answers, then call on pairs at random to collect eight to ten answers. Look at the answers and ask, "Do you remember that behaving actually has four parts: acting, thinking, feeling, and physiology? Which part is emphasized in these answers?" Tell students that you want them to do an activity to help them remember the four components of total behavior.

Cruising the Road

1. Tell the students that they will be doing this activity in their base groups.

2. Say, "I am going to assign a feeling, an emotion, to each base group. It will be the job of the group to brainstorm actions, thoughts, and physiology that combine with the feeling to make a total behavior. Each group will then dramatize its feeling—it will perform its acting, physiology, and thinking (by saying the thoughts out loud) for the rest of the class."

In this activity, students use their **bodily/kinesthetic** intelligence to dramatize a total behavior. They use their **interpersonal/social** intelligence to work together in small groups.

3. Tell students that each group will need a diarist to write down the thoughts, a choreographer to keep track of suggested actions, and a nurse to record suggested physical feelings that accompany the feeling. Review the LEARN guidelines.

4. Assign a feeling to each group, and then tell them that they have fifteen minutes to brainstorm their lists of actions, thoughts, and physical feelings and to practice acting out the actions and physiology. Encourage them to really ham it up. Tell them that the more dramatic the presentations are, the longer they will be remembered. Demonstrate a feeling for them. I like to use my fear of heights. I can really emote about my sweaty feet and hands, churning stomach, spaghetti legs, fear of being pulled over the edge, thoughts about what a fool I was to get myself into this position, and so on.

   Some feelings that I like to use with students are: pride, bashfulness, inclusion, sadness, exclusion, happiness, triumph, anger, contentment, jealousy, hopefulness, encouragement.

5. Call on students at random to summarize the instructions. Ask if they need any clarification.

6. Tell groups to form quickly and quietly. Do the brainstorming and practicing.

7. At the end of the allotted time, ask groups if they are finished. If they are not, ask how much more time they reasonably need.

8. When all groups are finished, ask if they want to volunteer to perform or if they want you to call on them at random. Have every group perform its dramatization for the rest of the class.

9. Thank the class for the wonderful performance when everyone is finished. Ask students to say a loud, warm thank you in unison. Direct the thank you.

Stopping to Think

Ask each student to write a personal journal entry that focuses on one personal feeling and the action, thinking, and physiology that combine with the feeling to make up a total behavior. Ask them to answer these questions: When I was using my bodily/kinesthetic (acting) behavior today, what was I thinking? What was I feeling? What was my body telling me? Was my body relaxed or clenched? What can I think and do to become more comfortable using this intelligence?

Activity #4

Total Behaviors and the Control Theory Track

Getting on the Road

This activity asks students and teachers to put a lot of pieces together and use them to understand the basis for behaviors and the creation of new behaviors. I ask the students to come back to this activity many times during the year. The more they practice using the control theory track, the better they understand their own behaviors. Teachers who have participated in an intensive week will recognize the track as a modification of Dr. Glasser's "blue chart." My students find the control theory track easier to use—they say that the one-way loop is easier for them to follow.

I *always* go through an example with the students before I ask them to "drive around" the track the first time. Doing this activity in small groups gives the students the opportunity to discuss the track and teach each other about it—and, as Dr. Glasser says, we learn 70 percent of what we discuss with each other and 95 percent of what we teach each other. This activity works best several weeks into the school year. Each group needs a sheet of chart paper and colored markers.

Hand out copies of the "Control Theory Track." Ask the students to follow the story you are telling on the track. Suggest that taking some notes may help them remember how the track and the story go together. I have a large track on chart paper that is posted on the blackboard as I tell the story, and I have a small car (with a key) that I can "drive" around the track. I also have "lightning bolts" that I can use to zap the car when the truck scales tilt. I tell the following story, moving the car around the track and making notes on the board as I do so.

senses

knowledge filter

Mike was walking in the woods with his parents one day. He saw orange metal diamonds on some trees, heard a drumming noise, and smelled a tangy smell.

Mike thought, "Those orange diamonds are trail markers. My parents are using them to stay on the trail. By staying on the

values filter/perceived world/
quality world

trail, we will not get lost. That's great! We'll get back home safe and sound. We'll be free from getting lost, have the power to find our way out of these woods, and get out healthy and alive." The orange trail markers are now in his perceived world. He knows what they are and has decided that they are positive—they will help him meet one or more of his genetic needs—so they are in the special place in his perceived world that is called the *quality world*.

arrowhead from
knowledge filter

gap between the knowledge
filter and values filter

"I don't know what the drumming noise is," he thought, and he tuned out the stamping of a partridge. "I wonder what that tangy smell is. Maybe I'll ask my mom about it. I sure am glad Mom and Dad are with me. They really know their way around the woods." Mike sees being with his mom and dad as helping to meet his survival and belonging needs. His mom and dad are pictures in his quality world.

senses

knowledge filter

values filter/
perceived world

comparing place

spin out
creating a new behavior

ineffective new
behavior—spin out

Mike turned to look at his parents and suddenly realized that he could no longer see them. He couldn't even hear their voices. "Oh, no! I'm alone! I don't want to be alone in the woods—I could get hurt or die! I want to be with my parents right now, but I'm all alone." Mike felt a wave of panic wash over him. He broke out in a cold sweat. He tried to scream, but all that he could manage was a strangled croaking noise. He had never been alone in the woods before. He ran blindly into the woods, thinking he might find a shortcut back to his parents. A loud crash in the woods ahead of him stopped him in his tracks. This time he really screamed.

creating and
organizing an
effective behavior

Mike thought, "Wait a minute. If I get back to the trail, I can just turn around and follow the orange diamonds. They do mark the trail going both ways." He could see his own panicked path through the woods and backtracked along it.

senses

knowledge filter

values filter/
perceived world/
quality world

comparing place/
in balance

creating/organizing an
effective behavior

Mike suddenly saw an orange diamond on a tree. Looking to his right, he saw two more and recognized the hill that he had climbed just before he realized his parents were "lost." He thought, "I've found the trail. Fantastic! I want a path back to my parents and out of the woods right now. This trail is just what I wanted to find. Now I can follow the orange markers back to safety."

Mike followed the trail back to the family car. There he found his parents, who were telling a forest ranger about their missing child. They, too, had been driving on the control theory track—but that's another story.

IRI/Skylight Training and Publishing, Inc.

Cruising the Road

In this activity, students use their **visual/ spatial** intelligence to follow the control theory track and to produce storyboards. They use their **verbal/ linguistic** intelligence to explain behaviors and their **interpersonal/ social** intelligence to work in small groups.

1. Tell the students that you are going to ask them to interpret their own stories using the control theory track. Tell them that coming to class prepared the next day will mean they have a story in mind. Suggest that children's stories (*Goldilocks and the Three Bears, The Three Little Pigs, Little Red Riding Hood*) or comic strips like "Calvin and Hobbes" are good sources of stories. Stress that their stories do *not* need to be original. You are just asking them to have the details of a story firmly in mind when they come to class the next day.

2. The next day, tell the students they will be working in small groups to interpret a story that *one* of them brought to class. They will interpret the story by telling where the action fits on the control theory track.

3. Tell the students that they will be doing a *storyboard* that tells their story in words and pictures and shows where the action is on the control theory track in words and pictures. Tell them that a storyboard is like a comic strip—ask if any of them have seen an example from advertising or filmmaking. Spend some time answering their questions about the storyboard. Emphasize the idea that graphics in this class need not be "great art."

4. Tell the students that each group will spend the first few minutes deciding which story to use. Tell them that each group may choose an artist to lightly sketch the illustrations in pencil, a calligrapher to write the words, and a colorizer to fill in the color once the artist has finished the sketch.

5. Groups will finish the storyboard in thirty minutes. Remind them that they need to focus on how the story "tracks." Where is each frame on the control theory track?

6. Ask the students to review the task. Call on the students at random to describe what the groups will be doing. Assign the groups and have them get together quickly and quietly. One person from each group will pick up a large sheet of paper and colored markers for the group.

7. Help groups keep track of time. Ask them to put away the markers at the end of the thirty minutes.

8. Ask the groups if they want to volunteer to present their storyboards or if they want you to call on them at random.

9. After the groups present their storyboards, meet briefly with each group. Help them fine-tune their understanding of the control theory track.

10. Ask group members to shake hands and thank each other after they have hung up their storyboard on the wall in the room.

Stopping to Think

Ask the students to record their thoughts about the following in their journals: Describe *effective control* and link it to responsible behavior. How do you feel when you are in effective control? What might you be thinking? Describe your physiology. Complete the following analogy: Effective Control is like Silly Putty because. . . . Name a song that reminds you of being in effective control. Do a sketch that shows effective control. Describe your comfort level in using your visual/spatial intelligence to do a storyboard. Sketch your comfort level. Describe your comfort level in using your social intelligence.

The Control Theory Track

The control theory track is a gameboard. It is not a static picture. It is a track that is used to explain behavior and the brain as a control system. The following steps explain what happens in the control theory track. (The explanation is written in first person to stress that each of us controls our own behavior.)

1. As I use a behavior, my five senses take in information about what is happening in the real world.

2. That information passes through my knowledge filter where I identify it as familiar or new, important or unimportant.

3. The information then passes through my values filter where it is identified as positive (quality world WANT) or neutral/negative (perceived world). Positive behavior meets one or more of my basic needs: survival, belonging, power, freedom, and fun.

4. Once the information passes through both filters, it becomes a GET.

5. The information passes on to the comparing place. GET is compared to WANT.

6. If GET is quality (see number 3): if GET equals WANT, I feel good. My behavior is effective, and I will continue to use it to get this want.

7. If GET is perceived (see number 3): if "GET" does not equal WANT, I feel bad. My scales tilt. My behavior is not effective. I will try a different behavior to see if it gets me what I want.

8. If the new behavior works, I will keep it (I will *organize* it). If the new behavior does not work, I will "spin out."

9. I will keep trying different behaviors until one gets me what I want. I may need to learn a new behavior. I may need help.

10. I always control for input. I always control to get what I want.

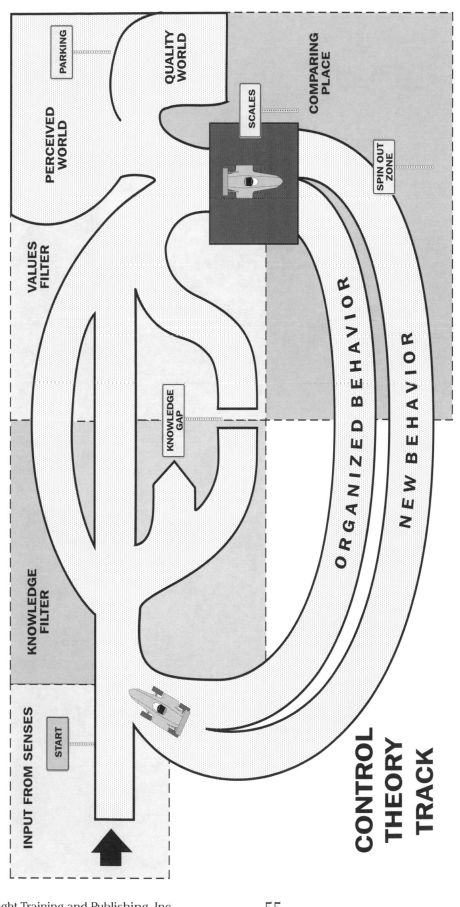

• Part III •

Following the Road to Success

Self-Evaluating and Planning for Quality Learning

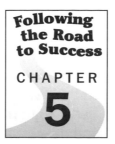
Determining the Destination

Getting to Quality Learning

Activity #1

An Overview of the Quality Learning Process

Getting on the Road

The "Quality Learning Road Map" in this section is a tool for teachers that I share with students very late in the year (if at all). It illustrates the route students follow in becoming quality learners, which ultimately leads to developing learning skills that add quality to their lives overall. I show the students this map late in the year because I believe showing it to them too early might discourage those who come to me with poor academic records and personal expectations of failure. I use the road map to help me identify where students are in the quality learning cycle and where they might choose to go next. I invite students who move directly to the top of the map after the first test to become my "assistants," the concurrent evaluation "experts" who help me during testing and the content "experts" in cooperative learning groups. I find that students are very willing to assume these roles for teachers they trust—after all, being an in-class "expert" can be very need satisfying. I have seen wonderful growth and development of learning skills in students who have chosen to follow the classroom experts who are using the road map. The students begin to parallel the experts' growth and development of leadership and communication skills. This is truly a win/win classroom strategy.

The real "hook" for using this tool effectively is starting at the very bottom of the map—establishing the climate for quality. The activities from parts one and two of this book fill the bottom two steps on the map. Those two steps take time to cover. You may want to think of them as your ten-mile-per-hour zone.

Skipping them, however, may weaken the rest of the roadbed. If the climate for quality is not in place and if students do not accept responsibility for their own actions, their self-evaluation and planning may not be as powerful (or, perhaps, as honest). The greatest growth results from thoughtful, honest self-evaluation. The payoff for taking the time to establish trust and teach control theory yields more rapid improvement in the quality of student learning.

Cruising the Road

1. Begin by establishing a warm, trusting environment that nurtures quality.

2. Teach students some control theory. Their understanding of control theory will grow along with their improvement as learners—you can use some of the road map steps to teach or reinforce control theory ideas.

3. About one-and-a-half weeks before the first content test of the year, have a class meeting in which you ask students to share with the rest of the class what they do to prepare for a test. My students like to answer in generalities: "I study really hard." I ask them to define their answers in terms of total behaviors. What do they do when they study? What do they think? Are they aware of their feelings? I tell students what content will be covered on the test. I ask them, "Why do you take tests in school? What is the purpose of testing?" We develop the idea that tests are tools used to measure how much students have learned.

4. I ask students what "learning" means. Does it mean memorizing, or does it mean being able to apply, analyze, and predict?

We eventually agree that learning can include all of these things. Some memorizing may be necessary, but being able to see the meaning of what is memorized gives learning its usefulness. I tell students that they will be asked to use what they learn in this class. I give them a list of "doing" verbs that are classified according to Bloom's taxonomy. Then I ask them, "What verbs ask you to gather (or memorize) information? What verbs ask you to process? What verbs ask you to apply or predict or synthesize information?" We discuss the differences in thinking skills that are involved in answering the different types of questions.

In this activity, students use their **verbal/linguistic** and **intrapersonal/ introspective** intelligences to write a learning plan. They use their **logical/ mathematical** intelligence to analyze the effectiveness of the plan.

5. I ask students to help me write questions for the test. Their questions are to be turned in to me about a week before the actual date of the test. Writing test questions is a good way of reviewing the material. It is not required—students may earn bonus points for writing test questions, however, and writing good questions helps students review the material.

6. The first test is a paper-and-pencil test. Before students turn in the test, I tell them that they may also earn a small bonus by self-evaluating the quality of their preparation. I give them a model, like the following: "I studied long and hard for this test. I know that I did the best job of test preparation I could. I learned a lot about the topic, so even if my letter grade is not an A, I will be happy that I studied as hard as I did." I tell them, "If you choose to self-evaluate, please be honest. You will earn the bonus no matter what you say. If you say that you did not study very much, that may be honest. You are evaluating the quality of your preparation to help yourself—not to please me."

7. The day after students take the individual test, I ask them to retake the test in cooperative learning groups. They retake the test before they see their individual test scores. I tell them that every student in every team that earns a score of 100 percent on the retest will earn back some percentage (usually 25 percent) of the points that he or she missed on the individual test. The retest is open book and notes, and teams that choose to do so may scout with other teams or with me for help. I move from team to team, asking students to explain why their teams chose the answers they did. That encourages students to discuss answers and explain them to each other rather than just letting the "expert" in the team fill out the answers.

8. When the team test is turned in, the members of the team may then look over their individual tests. I answer any questions that the students may have about their individual tests, and then I ask them to reevaluate the quality of their test preparation and learning.

9. The day after the first team test, I say to students, "Now you have had a chance to test the effectiveness of your study habits—your learning plans—for this class. Let's take some time to figure out how to remember what was successful or how to strengthen what may have been weak."

10. We do a think/pair/share using the question, "What does an A student who is doing quality learning do? What does that look like and sound like?" I give each student a blank copy of the "An 'A' Student Doing Quality Learning" chart so that he or she may keep track of the answers. I have included a set of sample answers for your information. Filling in this chart as a whole class helps weaker students by suggesting new learning behaviors that they may want to reorganize and use.

11. After the think/pair/share, I tell students, "If you want to, you may use this information to write up a personal learning plan." I have a large blank copy of "Doing a Quality Job as a Learner" on chart paper that I post on the blackboard. I ask students for ideas about each box on the chart. After we have given everyone a chance to contribute their ideas, I give each student a blank copy of the chart. I tell them that they can earn a small bonus if they do personal learning plans and show them to me before the next test. I stress that doing the plan is not required.

12. We go through another learning/testing cycle. Sometimes the test is a traditional paper-and-pencil test. As a high school chemistry teacher, I believe that part of my job is to help my college-bound students become better test-takers. It will be useful learning for them in the very near future. Sometimes the test is a concurrent evaluation. (For a description of concurrent evaluation, see *The Quality School Teacher* by Dr. William Glasser.) My students usually find the first concurrent evaluation of the year more threatening than a regular test. The idea of meeting with me (or another expert) face to face and demonstrating their knowledge is scary. For that reason, I do not use concurrent evaluation right away. I wait until trust has been established in the classroom. Some teachers have asked, "What about the

experts? Do they let their classmates get away with murder? How can you trust students to do a good job of testing other students?" My answer is that the climate for quality takes care of those potential problems. The experts want to be trusted. They feel very powerful and free from suspicion. Being an expert is very need satisfying, and the experts do not want to lose that trust, belonging, power, and freedom.

13.   After the test or concurrent evaluation cycle, students are asked to self-evaluate the effectiveness of their learning plans and to revise those plans to make them more effective. Any student may also self-evaluate as they did after the first test. Because students who are evaluating and revising learning plans are doing more work, their bonus is larger. My students are very aware of the desirability of getting high grades. Larger bonuses are very attractive to them and influence many of them to do personal learning plans.

14.   Any student may join the learning plan/evaluation/revision cycle at any time during the school year. Some students may doubt that doing a learning plan is useful, at least at first. As they see their classmates improving as learners, they may decide that there is something to this learning plan business after all. I keep the door open for the those students. It is not my job to judge them or to accuse them of not caring about their learning. Many of my students have been so discouraged for so long, they need time to see that a new strategy may have some merit for them.

15.   I never change learning plans. I may ask questions about them, but I never tamper with them. The learning plan is the student's personal property.

16.   I do encourage students to continue to self-evaluate all year long. Students who are happy with their learning plans often tell me that self-evaluation helps them see how well they used their learning plans and what roadblocks may have gotten in their way. They use this knowledge to plan ways around those roadblocks.

Stopping to Think

Ask students to complete the following self-evaluation in their journals: "Developing good learning skills has added quality to my life. . . ." Encourage them to keep this tool out at all times. Stress the importance of self-evaluation and planning as tools for personal growth. Find ways to model this for students as you move through the year. Ask students if they can identify the intelligences they use as they develop and revise their learning plans. Check their understanding and help them with the identification if you need to.

Quality Learning Road Map

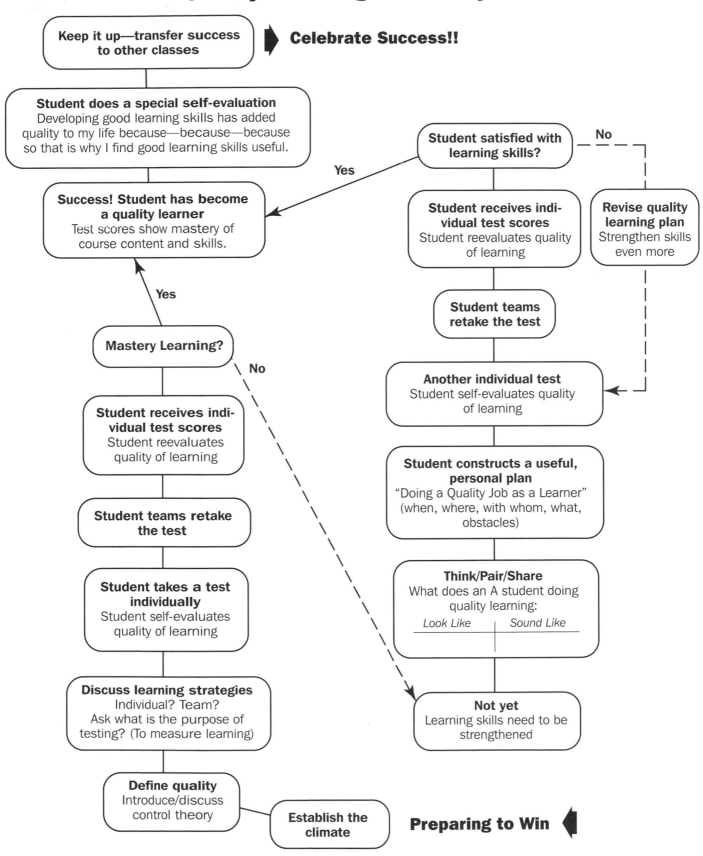

Keep it up—transfer success to other classes

Celebrate Success!!

Student does a special self-evaluation
Developing good learning skills has added quality to my life because—because—because so that is why I find good learning skills useful.

Student satisfied with learning skills?

No

Yes

Success! Student has become a quality learner
Test scores show mastery of course content and skills.

Student receives individual test scores
Student reevaluates quality of learning

Revise quality learning plan
Strengthen skills even more

Student teams retake the test

Yes

Mastery Learning?

No

Another individual test
Student self-evaluates quality of learning

Student receives individual test scores
Student reevaluates quality of learning

Student constructs a useful, personal plan
"Doing a Quality Job as a Learner" (when, where, with whom, what, obstacles)

Student teams retake the test

Student takes a test individually
Student self-evaluates quality of learning

Think/Pair/Share
What does an A student doing quality learning:

Look Like	Sound Like

Discuss learning strategies
Individual? Team?
Ask what is the purpose of testing? (To measure learning)

Not yet
Learning skills need to be strengthened

Define quality
Introduce/discuss control theory

Establish the climate

Preparing to Win

AN "A" STUDENT DOING QUALITY LEARNING

Looks Like	Sounds Like
Doing the assigned reading	Quiet
Writing a summary	Talking about content
Working math/science problems	Quizzing other students
Rewriting answers to homework questions	Being quizzed by other students
Reading class notes	Nondistracting music
Writing a summary of notes/reading	Phoning a friend for help
Outlining/mapping/webbing information	Asking the teacher for help
Alone	Paraphrasing
Small groups	Checking for understanding
Sitting at a desk/table	Encouraging each other
Good light	Teaching/explaining
Good attendance	"I understand"
Writing a review sheet	"I know this"
Getting plenty of sleep	"What questions could she ask us?"

IRI/Skylight Training and Publishing, Inc.

AN "A" STUDENT DOING QUALITY LEARNING

Looks Like	Sounds Like

DOING A QUALITY JOB AS A LEARNER

A Personal Plan

Co-verified by (a friend)	Evaluated (when)	Success Celebrated by (how)

WITH WHOM will I learn?

by myself
with a friend
with a teacher
with a brother/sister
with a parent
with a small group of "like-minded" students
with a tutor
or??

WHERE will I learn?

in the classroom
in the school library
at the public library
at home (what room or rooms)
in the cafeteria
in the tutorial center
at a friend's house

or??

WHAT will I do to learn?

read/reread the book
read/reread my notes
take notes
work out solutions to examples in the book
make note of questions that I have
do webs/mind maps/outlines as I read
teach others what I am learning
ask for help
clear up misunderstandings   or??

WHEN will I learn?

the night before a test
during my "free" periods
during breaks at work
before school
during my lunch period
evenings
weekends

or??   **NOW!!!**

~~Later?~~

ROADBLOCKS How can I get around them?

What is realistic?
What is reasonable?
What might distract me? (television, radio, stereo, phone, the dog, little sisters/brothers, friends)
Do I need a written schedule?

or??

DOING A QUALITY JOB AS A LEARNER

A Personal Plan

Co-verified by (a friend)	Evaluated (when)	Success Celebrated by (how)

WHEN will I learn?

WHERE will I learn?

WITH WHOM will I learn?

NOW!!!

Later?

ROADBLOCKS How can I get around them?

WHAT will I do to learn?

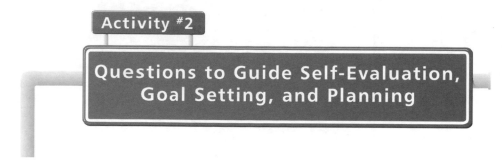

Activity #2

Questions to Guide Self-Evaluation, Goal Setting, and Planning

Getting on the Road

My students are not natural self-evaluators. To them, evaluation has come to mean judging, excusing, and blaming. When I ask them to self-evaluate without giving them any initial guidance, they say things like, "I should have . . . ," "I could have . . . ," or "I couldn't do it because. . . ." I need a tool to help them get out of the excusing, blaming, and judging rut and into true self-evaluation. Students use this tool individually and privately. Each student needs one copy of the "Weekly Reflections" sheet.

Ask students to think about a personal goal for the class for the following week. Then ask them, "Do you have a 'formula' that you can use to help you reach that goal? Do you think that you can reach your goal? I want to show you a tool that you can use to help you reach your personal goals."

Cruising the Road

1. At the end of a school week, give each student a "Weekly Reflections" sheet. Tell them to focus on the "Think and Decide" section. They cannot use the "Look at Your Goal" section until the second week in the cycle.

2. Go through an example as they look through the questions. Here is what I use as an example: "(1) Next week, I want to have more fun in class. (2) To have more fun in class, I need to think of ways to have fun that will not totally disrupt learning. (3) I am willing to look at new or different behaviors that will help me have more fun. (4) I need to do something different, because I am not having as much fun as I want to. (5) Some new behaviors that might be helpful are telling more puns, showing a cartoon a day on the overhead projector, asking you to volunteer to tell jokes (in good taste), or learning more about real-world uses of the topic we are discussing. (6) Maybe you can help me

IRI/Skylight Training and Publishing, Inc.

In this activity, students use their **intrapersonal/ introspective** and **logical/ mathematical** intelligences to self-evaluate the effectiveness of their behaviors. They use their **verbal/ linguistic** intelligence to write their self-evaluations and goal plans.

think of other ways to have fun that will also enhance learning. (7) I will pick one new behavior and start using it on Monday. (8) In fact, I will start showing a cartoon a day on Monday. To do that, I need to select five cartoons from my collection, enlarge them, make a transparency of each one, and have them ready to show on time. I also need to have an overhead projector in the classroom. Some roadblocks that may get in my way are being 'too busy' to do the enlarging or make the transparencies or forgetting the overhead projector. To get around them, I will schedule time into two of my free hours for the enlarging and transparency making (in case the machines are busy) and put a note on my desk reminding me to get the overhead projector. (9) I will ask you to help me keep track of showing the cartoons. If I have remembered all of them on Friday, I will celebrate by asking you for a round of applause."

3. Ask students if they have any questions about the questions. Help them understand what you are asking them to do.

4. Take time to look at "Some Areas for Goal Setting." Be sure students understand the difference between a goal and a plan. A goal is a destination. A plan describes the behaviors that are going to be used to get there. Students may pick a destination for the list on the "Goal Setting" sheet. A student may say, for example, "I want to be more prompt. I want to get to each class at least thirty seconds before the tardy bell rings." Another student might say, "I want to be more respectful; I want to demonstrate my respect for others through my actions and words." A third student might say, "I want to improve my preparation for class; I want to come to class with all of the materials I need, and I want to be ready to contribute my fair share." These are goals. The specific behaviors that students say they will use to reach these goals are their action plans. The second student might say, "To demonstrate respect for others, I will say 'please' and 'thank you'; I will yield to others going through doorways; I will take my turn at the end of the cafeteria line; I will say 'excuse me'; and I will go with the flow of traffic (not push or shove)."

5. After you go over an example, give students three to five minutes to go through the "Think and Decide" questions on the "Weekly Reflections" sheet. Ask them to write out their personal goals and plans in their journals.

6. At the end of the following week, ask students to get out the "Weekly Reflections" sheets. Ask them to help you self-evaluate by going through the "Look at Your Goal" questions. Go through your answers with the students; emphasize the last item. Self-evaluation does not mean judging, blaming, or excusing. Self-evaluation means figuring out where you are and if you are happy being there. Remind students of the scales in the control theory track. Tell them that they are really asking themselves, "Am I getting what I want?" If the answer is yes, they may choose to continue to use their present behaviors. If the answer is no, they may choose to find new behaviors and reorganize those behaviors to get what they want.

Stopping to Think

Encourage students to continue the weekly cycle. I build "Weekly Reflections" in to the planning and self-evaluation bonus system discussed in activity 1 of this chapter. Ask students to self-evaluate their ability to use their intrapersonal intelligence. Ask if they are becoming more confident in their self-evaluation. Ask if they need help.

IRI/Skylight Training and Publishing, Inc.

WEEKLY REFLECTIONS

Look at Your Goal

What was your goal for this week?

Did you reach that goal?

What did you do to reach that goal?

What specific actions and thoughts were most helpful in reaching your goal?

What specific actions and thoughts were the greatest obstacles to reaching your goal?

How did you get around these obstacles?

Did you do the best that you could in this class this week? (No excuses—just answer the question for yourself.)

Think and Decide

What is your goal for this class for next week?

What do you need to do to reach that goal?

What are you willing to do to reach that goal?

Do you need to change your behavior to reach your goal?

Do you know what new behaviors would be helpful?

Who do you see helping you to learn new behaviors?

When will you change your behaviors?

What is your plan for reaching your goal?

How will you know when you reach your goal? How will you celebrate?

SOME AREAS FOR GOAL SETTING

Academic

Grades

Quality of preparation for class

Quality of "hardcopy" work

Notebook/log/journal

Test/quiz performance

And?

Personal (effective, responsible) Behavior

Attendance

Prompness

Acknowledging responsibility (avoiding blaming and excusing)

Keeping "cool"

Maintaining focus

And?

Interpersonal Behavior

Respect

Cooperation

"Putting up" (not putting down)

Tolerance

Listening

Sharing

Helping

And?

Activity #3

Characteristics of a Good Plan

Getting on the Road

Many students who want to do learning plans have had little or no experience in developing any kind of action plan. To help them develop good plans, I use an activity that engages them in defining the characteristics of a good plan. I survey my classes before setting up the groups for this activity to identify students who are musically talented, and I try to have at least one "musical" person in each group. If a class is short on musical members, I substitute with "poets." The activity is designed to use eight groups of three or more students.

I begin this activity by telling students that I remember vividly the 1985 Chicago Bears. That was the team that won the Super Bowl some weeks after coming out with the "Super Bowl Shuffle" video. I have a copy of the video, and I show the first chorus and the first few verses to the class. (In case you are not familiar with this shuffle, it uses a rap rhythm.) Then I ask them if the shuffle helps them remember who the players are and what positions they played on that team. I tell them that we will be creating our own shuffle to help all of us remember the characteristics of a good plan. I perform this chorus for them:

> We are the School Learning Crew
>
> Making our plans—seeing them through.
>
> We are good and we're improving—
>
> Our plans have us really grooving!
>
> If you want to write your own plan,
>
> Learn this shuffle and then you can.

Cruising the Road

In this activity, students use their **musical/rhythmic** intelligence to write and perform a "shuffle," and their **interpersonal/ social** intelligence to work in small groups.

1. Tell the students that they will be working in small groups. Tell them that these groups will be formed around an "expert" musician.

2. Tell the students that their job will be to write and perform a shuffle verse about some characteristic of a good plan. Tell them to use the format—rhythm and rhyme scheme—of the verse you gave them. Put the verse on the blackboard or on an overhead projector so students can refer to it as needed.

3. List the characteristics of an effective plan on the board or on chart paper. Discuss them with the class as a whole—be sure that students know what each characteristic means before assigning the groups or asking them to write the verses. The characteristics are:

    Simple: A good plan is not complicated. It consists of logical steps that take a reasonable amount of time.

    Specific: A good plan tells what you will do, when you will do it, who you will do it with, how often you will do it, and what time of day you will do it—it is so detailed that you can visualize yourself doing it as if it were a movie.

    Positive: A good plan tells what you will do, not what you will stop doing. It is a plan that you can do, not one that asks you to do things beyond your level of expertise. A good plan is what you plan to do.

    Independent: A good plan can be done by yourself. You may choose to include someone else, but you don't need anyone else to carry out your plan.

    Immediate: A good plan is something that you can and will start doing right away. It is what you will do today, not tomorrow or next week.

    Reinforcing: You feel good when you follow your plan. It gets you what you want. You will organize and reuse this plan because it is effective.

    Repetitive: A good plan works over and over again. You don't need to make a new study plan for each new unit of study or each different content area. A good plan will work for all of your mastery learning wants.

    Requires commitment: You pledge that you will do this plan. You commit your-self to taking this course of action. You say, "I will do this!," and you do it.

4. Go back to the instructions for the task. Call on students at random to summarize or paraphrase the instructions for writing the rap verse.

5. Assign the students to their groups. Tell them that you will finish giving the instructions for the task and assign each group its characteristic after the groups have gotten together. Have the students move into their groups quickly and quietly.

 IRI/Skylight Training and Publishing, Inc.

6. After the groups have formed, tell the students, "Groups will have twenty minutes to write and rehearse the verses. Each group needs a timekeeper to help the group finish on time, a composer to write the verse down, and a conductor to keep the group on task. After the 'write and practice' time, each group will perform its verse for the rest of the class. Groups will perform in the order in which the characteristics are listed on the board."

Ask the students how they want you to assign a characteristic to each group. My students often wanted to volunteer for characteristics. I also have each characteristic and its definition printed on a slip of paper. If students do not want to volunteer for characteristics, I ask groups to draw them out of a "hat."

7. As soon as all groups have received a characteristic, tell them to start writing and practicing.

8. After twenty minutes, ask groups if they are all finished. If they are not, ask how much more time they realistically think they need.

9. Start with the whole class "shuffling" the chorus. Then have each group stand and perform its verse. End with the whole class doing the shuffle again. Do a round of applause for the great performance.

Stopping to Think

Ask each group to self-evaluate by answering these questions as a group: What was our best action today? What was our best thought? What would we strengthen next time we work together?

Ask each individual to self-evaluate by answering these questions: What is the greatest strength of my personal learning plan? What do I need to strengthen? How comfortable did I feel using my musical/rhythmic intelligence? What can I do to become more comfortable?

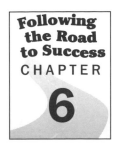
Give 'Em a Brake

Evaluation of Behaviors and Grades

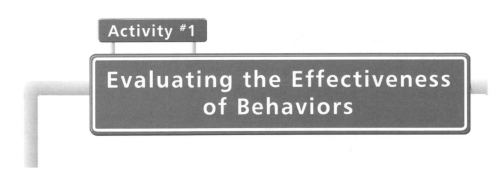

Activity #1

Evaluating the Effectiveness of Behaviors

Getting on the Road

Self-evaluation of behaviors can help students lead more effective, responsible lives both in and out of the classroom. I like to help students develop a "gimmick" they can use, quickly and individually, to evaluate the effectiveness of their behaviors at any time. I tell them that the frustration signal they feel from time to time may be telling them they are not getting what they want. The heart of self-evaluation is looking at what they are doing and asking, "Is what I am doing working? Is it getting me what I want to get when I use this behavior? How important is it to me to get what I thought I wanted? Do I need to try a different behavior?" Self-evaluation is the key to changing behaviors in an effective, responsible direction.

I know that students may not understand the abstract, so I give them a specific example of self-evaluation leading to a different behavior. I tell them this story: In 1976, I went to the Summer Olympics in Montreal with my husband and some friends of ours. On our first morning in Montreal, we all went out to breakfast at a restaurant where, we soon found out, the table help did not speak or understand English. For the most part, that was not a problem. The menu was printed in French and English, so we found the description of what we wanted on the menu and pointed to that description when the waitress came to take the order. After we had placed the order and the waitress had taken back the menus, one of our friends remembered that he had wanted to order a glass of milk but had forgotten to do so. He waved to the waitress, and she came back to the table. He said, in English, "I want a glass of milk with my breakfast." She gave him a blank look. He said it again, louder and slower. She looked at him even more blankly. He knew that he was not getting what he wanted—his glass of milk—using words, so he picked up his glass of water and pointed. He had drunk most of his water. The waitress showed us an "ah-ha!" look, left, and returned with a pitcher of ice water. Our friend, knowing that once again he was not getting what he wanted, started tugging at his hair and rolling his eyes. Finally, with an "ah-ha!" look of his own, he seized his glass, pointed at it, and loudly mooed. The waitress laughed, nodded, and left. When she returned, she was carrying a glass of milk. The final behavior worked. Everyone was happy.

The students and I summarize the behaviors and their effectiveness:

> Talking: didn't work; try again.
> Talking louder: didn't work; try again.
> Pointing to glass: didn't work; try again.
> Pointing to glass and mooing: worked; do again.

I tell students that change results from comparing what we want with what we are getting, finding out that we are not getting what we want, and looking for some other behavior to try.

Cruising the Road

1. Do a think/pair/share. Ask students to think of a nursery rhyme song (like "Farmer in the Dell" or "She'll Be Coming 'Round the Mountain"). Give individuals ten seconds to think of an answer. Give partners twenty seconds to slide together and exchange answers. Call on randomly selected pairs for song titles. Collect a list of six to eight song titles.

2. Tell students that they will do this activity in base groups. Tell them that each group will do a song about self-evaluation and behavior. The song will include a reference to behavior (doing), comparing wants with gets, keeping effective behaviors, and changing ineffective behaviors.

3. Tell students that each group will do actions that demonstrate the song as they sing it. Demonstrate for them.

In this activity, students will use their **musical/rhythmic** intelligence to compose and perform a song about self-evaluating behaviors. They will use their **bodily/kinesthetic** intelligence to pantomime the song and their **interpersonal/ social** intelligence to work in small groups.

(sung to the tune of "Farmer in the Dell")

Words	Action(s)
I'm doing what I do	*Picking apples*
To get a want or two	*Picking apples*
I'm getting them; I'm getting them!	*Scales balancing*
I'm keeping what I do.	*Picking apples*
I'm doing what I do	*Waving arms*
To get a want or two	*Waving arms*
But I'm not getting what I want.	*Scales out of balance*
I'm changing what I do.	*"You're out!" sign*

4. Tell students that they may use one of the nursery rhyme tunes from the list or they may think of a different one, but they are to use a nursery rhyme tune.

5. Check for understanding. Call on students at random to summarize or paraphrase the instructions.

6. Tell students that groups will have fifteen minutes to write, choreograph, and practice the songs. Songs will be performed for the whole class.

7. Ask groups to form quickly and quietly and do the songs.

8. After fifteen minutes, ask groups if they are ready to perform. Ask how much more time they realistically need.

9. When all groups are ready, ask if they want to volunteer to perform or if they want you to call on them at random. Be sure that every group has a chance to perform.

10. Lead the class in standing and saying "Thank you!" to someone else in the class.

Stopping to Think

Ask students if they remember acting out a nursery rhyme song when they were in an elementary grade. I tell my students that "Farmer in the Dell" is one that I remember doing in kindergarten—and I remember how everyone wanted to be the cheese and get to "ham it up" alone. I tell them that the combination of musical/rhythmic and bodily/kinesthetic intelligences can be a powerful one when we are inventing memory gimmicks. I ask them to write a personal journal entry about a similar experience that they remember from an early grade. I also ask them to summarize what they have learned about self-evaluation and how it can lead to change.

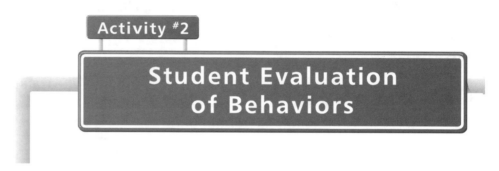

Activity #2

Student Evaluation of Behaviors

Getting on the Road

Often, students may want to use more-effective behaviors in the classroom, but they do not know what those behaviors might be. These individual tools give students ideas about effective, responsible behaviors and a way of self-evaluating their use of those behaviors. I use these tools as part of the students' personal paper trails that they use to determine their grades at the end of a grading period. Each student needs one copy each of the "Quality Learner," "Quality Teammate," and "Team Self-Evaluation Questions" sheets.

To help students evaluate themselves as quality learners, ask them, "What behaviors lead to success in school? What do good students do that helps them earn good grades?" Have a class meeting to collect answers to the questions. Record the students answers on the blackboard. Do this before students see the "Evaluating Myself as a Quality Learner" sheet.

To help students evaluate themselves as quality teammates, ask them, "What behaviors are used by successful team players? What are some reasons for learning to be a good team player?" Have a class meeting to collect answers to the questions. Record student answers on the blackboard. Do this before students see the "Evaluating Myself as a Quality Teammate" sheet.

I do not use any special lead-in to help students evaluate themselves as a team until after they have been encouraged to do the individual forms a few times. I ask members of cooperative learning groups to fill out one copy of the form after they have worked together.

Cruising the Road

In this activity, students use their **verbal/ linguistic** intelligence to develop a list of effective behaviors and their **intrapersonal/ introspective** intelligence to self-evaluate their personal use of those behaviors.

1. Give each student a copy of whichever form corresponds to the class discussion question.

2. Compare the student-generated list of student behaviors with the behaviors on the form. (I found very good agreement between student-generated lists and the form, which was a composite of a number of student lists.)

3. Ask students if they want to substitute any of their ideas (from the list on the blackboard) for the ideas on the form. Tell them that individuals may make their own substitutions. Encourage them to tailor the form to their personal, individual needs.

4. Tell students that part of their grade in your class at the end of the grading period will be based on their effective use of responsible behaviors and that you will ask to see a "paper trail"—a self-evaluation record of their uses of responsible behavior that they have kept throughout the grading period. Tell them that some of them may want to learn new behaviors that will help them become better students/teammates and that these forms will give them some suggestions about behaviors they can use.

5. If a student asks, "Do I have to use the form?," answer, "No, but I will want to see an ongoing self-evaluation of your behaviors at the end of the grading period."

6. Encourage students to set up a grid on their own paper that they can use to keep track of their "smilies." Tell them that they will get one copy of the printed form to use as a self-evaluation guide. Suggest a grid with spaces that will allow them to record a self-evaluation at the end of each week (grid on page 89).

7. When the time for grades arrives, ask to see a weekly self-evaluation of learner/teammate behaviors during your grade conference with each student.

8. Give the team self-evaluation to each cooperative learning group toward the end of a period the group spent working together. Ask that all members discuss the answers together, sign the sheet, and give it to you before they leave class. Make note of what teams say about how they would like the teacher to help them. Return the forms to the teams.

Stopping to Think

You may choose to check on self-evaluation of behaviors several times during the grading period. I also fill out a form for each student for one specific day during the grading period. That way the student and I can compare notes about our perceptions of behaviors. If the student says, "But you got me on a bad day!," I ask, "Do you have bad days often? Do you see yourself as a bad-day person or a good-day person?" That can lead to interesting dialogue and more self-evaluation. I also ask students if they feel more confident in their use of introspective intelligence and if they are choosing to use this intelligence to self-evaluate outside the classroom.

EVALUATING MYSELF AS A QUALITY LEARNER

Use this document to honestly evaluate your behaviors in class this week.

	You Bet! (2)	So-So (1)	Not Yet! (0)
I was in class every day.			
I was ready to start on time every day.			
I was courteous to all speakers—I listened and learned when others were talking.			
I came to class prepared.			
I asked others for help—not answers.			
I did a good job of taking notes and gathering information.			
I asked good questions.			
I persisted in completing tasks and getting answers to my questions or solving problems.			
I really focused on daily lessons and tasks.			
I was in effective control of my behavior—I felt good about my behavior.			

EVALUATING MYSELF AS A QUALITY TEAMMATE

Use this document to honestly evaluate your participation in assigned groups in this class at the end of each week.

	You Bet! (2)	So-So (1)	Not Yet! (0)
I stayed with my group(s) physically and mentally.	☺	☺	☹
I helped my group(s) stay on task.	☺	☺	☹
I remembered to use my very quiet voice.	☺	☺	☹
I came to class prepared.	☺	☺	☹
I asked others for help—not answers.	☺	☺	☹
I helped my teammates by sharing my information and insights.	☺	☺	☹
I encouraged everyone to participate in our task.	☺	☺	☹
I checked to be sure my teammates agreed with and understood what we were doing.	☺	☺	☹
I remembered to thank my teammates for their help and to help them celebrate our successes.	☺	☺	☹
I collected information for absent teammates.	☺	☺	☹

IRI/Skylight Training and Publishing, Inc.

TEAM SELF-EVALUATION QUESTIONS

Teams will collaborate on developing thoughtful answers to these questions after working together in class.

Today, we were asked to (do what?) . . .

Our best actions were . . .

Our best thoughts were . . .

We helped each other learn and succeed by . . .

Next time we want to strengthen (what acting or thinking skills?) . . .

We would like the teacher to help us by . . .

This activity helped us meet the following needs (describe specifically how the activity helped team members meet their needs):

Power:

Fun:

Freedom:

Belonging:

Overall, we feel that our performance today was . . .

Brain Dead	**OK**	**Awesome**

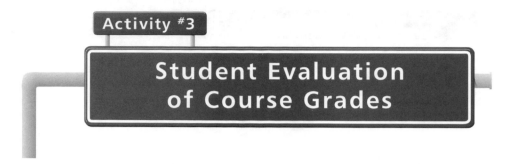

Activity #3

Student Evaluation of Course Grades

Getting on the Road

Some students appear to believe that teachers have a magic formula for figuring out letter grades. As long as letter grades are a part of school, I believe that students can be given tools to help them know at any point in time just what letter grade they are earning. I find that teaching students how to use these tools gives them such good information that they do not argue or complain about their grades—they know exactly what the criteria are for earning a given letter grade and what they need to do to earn the grade of their choice. Students do their bookkeeping individually. Each student needs one copy of the "Course Rubric" and the "Self-Evaluation of Course Grade" sheet.

Students need to know what information is used to determine their class grades. They need to have tools for collecting or evaluating their own work. The "Evaluating Myself" tools discussed in activity 2 can be used to assess personal learning and teamwork behaviors week by week. The course rubric is possibly the most valuable tool for clarifying expectations and evaluating performance.

Cruising the Road

1. Tell the students that you want to take the mystery out of the grading process in your class. I say, "I am going to give you copies of all of the tools that I use to determine your grade in this class. I will help you learn how to use the tools. Then you will know at any time what your grade is in this class."

2. Give the students a copy of a rubric which clarifies the letter grade standards in a number of categories. The first three years that I used a rubric, I asked students for their ideas about the standards for letter grades. I now use a prewritten rubric and ask students to let me know if they want to change anything in the rubric. We agree on standards at the beginning of the year. That helps cut down on problems later on.

In this activity students use their **intrapersonal/introspective** and **logical/mathematical** intelligences to self-evaluate their work. They use their **visual/spatial** and **verbal/linguistic** intelligences to create self-evaluation tools.

3. Be very careful to return all tests, assignments, and project evaluations so that students have the information they need about those grades. Encourage students to keep a record of those scores and any other information they will need to use the rubric in figuring out their own grades.

4. Encourage the students to set up grids for their weekly self-evaluation of learning and teamwork behaviors. I suggest that the grid look like the one below.

Students fill in the dates and behaviors and record their self-evaluation (suggested point scores are "2" for "you bet!," "1" for "so-so," or "0" for "not yet," or they may choose to use "+" for "you bet," "✓" for "so-so," or "–" for "not yet.")

Behavior **Week ending**	9/5/95	9/12/95	9/19/95							
In class	2	1	2							
Prepared	0	1	2							
Good question	2	1	2							

5. Give each student a copy of the "Self-Evaluation of Course Grade" form. I tell students that academic work includes tests and quizzes, daily preparation, the daily log, class notes, projects, and concurrent evaluations. Teamwork skills have been self-evaluated using the weekly teamwork "smilies." Responsible behaviors have been self-evaluated using the quality learner "smilies."

6. Tell the students if and how you will "weigh" grades. In my class, each of the eight categories on the rubric and responsible behavior (not on the rubric) are weighted equally. This gives nine grades to average, which works well for me.

7. Tell the students the rules for figuring out their grades. Here are my rules: A student with an A average has all A's and B's. A student with a B average has all A's, B's, and C's; a student with a C average has no F's. Go over a few examples of figuring out grades.

8. Ask the students to fill out the "Self-Evaluation" form by a given date. Tell them that on that date, you will be ready to have a (very short) grade conference with each of them.

9. On the date, be ready to fill in the bottom portion of the "Self-Evaluation" form. Most of the time, students and I agree about their grades. When a student shows me the form, I just say, "I agree!" or "We're right on!" or "You bet!" I sign the form and return it to the student. If we disagree, I ask the student to come back later. After everyone else has had his or her grade conference, I get together with anyone whose grade estimate did not agree with mine, and we look over the evidence. At that time, I may ask to see the student's paper trail. I have my copies of my paper-trail documents handy. If the student's paper trail is missing or nonexistent, my paper trail wins by default.

10. You may choose to ask students to take the "Self-Evaluation" form home, have a parent sign it, and bring it back to show you the signature. This helps keep parents informed about grades and the ways in which those grades are determined.

11. Discuss with the students the intelligences that were used during the evaluation/grading process. Identify how the intelligences were used.

 IRI/Skylight Training and Publishing, Inc.

Stopping to Think

For students, closure comes when the teacher co-verifies the class grade by signing the "Self-Evaluation" form. The student-teacher contact involved in the process, no matter how brief, gives students ownership of their grades. Students have some responsibility for assessing their achievement in the class. Their involvement in the process helps them understand how grades are figured out and ends most of those dreaded end-of-term complaints and arguments about grades before they start. For me, as long as grades are a part of school, grading with students instead of grading for students is the only way to do the job.

COURSE RUBRIC

You decide. What grade do you want in this course? Are you doing what it takes to make the grade? What behaviors do you need to choose to get where you want to be?

	A	B	C	D	F
Tests and/or Quizzes	All scores equal to or above 80%.	All scores between 70% and 79%.	All scores between 60% and 69%.	All scores between 50% and 59%.	All scores less than 50%.
Daily Prep.	Well prepared 10 days out of every 10—come with all necessary work done.	Well prepared 9 days out of every 10—come with all necessary work done.	Well prepared 8 days out of every 10—come with all necessary work done.	Well prepared 6 days out of every 10—come with all necessary work done.	Well prepared every once in a while.
Daily Log	Every day starts a new page. Complete log-in and log-out every day.	Every day starts a new page. Complete log-in and log-out 9 days out of every 10.	Every day starts a new page. Complete log-in and log-out 8 days out of every 10.	Every day starts a new page. Complete log-in and log-out 6 days out of every 10.	Every day starts a new page. Complete log-in and log-out for a few days.
Class Notes	Quality notes for every day of class—all notes from board plus personal extras.	Quality notes for 9 days of every 10 in class—all notes from board plus personal extras.	Quality notes for 8 days of every 10 in class—all notes from board plus personal extras.	Quality notes for 6 days of every 10 in class—all notes from board plus personal extras.	Some notes for a few days of class.
Team Skills	Always on task and with team; rated helpful by teammates.	Always on task and with team; rated helpful by teammates 9 days out of 10.	Always on task and with team; rated helpful by teammates 8 days out of 10.	Always on task and with team; rated helpful by teammates 6 days out of 10.	Seldom on task or with team; rated helpful by teammates rarely.
Assignments	Always turned in on time; thoroughly and thoughtfully completed.	9 out of 10 turned in complete and on time.	8 out of 10 turned in on time; may need rewriting.	6 out of 10 turned in on time; most need rewriting.	Few if any turned in on time; usually need rewriting.
Concurrent Evaluation	100% score. Completed early. Is an "expert" who helps by questioning other students.	90% score. Completed early. Is an "expert" who helps by questioning other students.	80% to 100% score. Completed by the deadline. Does not question/test other students.	N/A	N/A
Project(s)	Meet at least 90% of criteria; done on time; rated by teammates as contributing "fair share" of the work.	Meet at least 80% to 89% of criteria; done on time; rated by teammates as contributing "fair share" of the work.	Meet at least 70% to 79% of criteria; done on time; rated by teammates as contributing "fair share" of the work.	Meet at least 60% to 69% of criteria; done on time; teammates say, "(S)he did some work."	Meet less than 60% of criteria; perhaps not finished on time; little or no contribution (if a team project).

IRI/Skylight Training and Publishing, Inc.

SELF-EVALUATION OF COURSE GRADE

_____   _____
              Name   *Date*

I believe my letter grade in this course is _____

because of these qualities of my academic work:

because of these qualities of my teamwork:

because of these responsible behaviors:

My completed weekly self-evaluations form the paper trail that I used in this self-evaluation.

                                        _____
                                                  Student Signature

▬ ▬

My records show that you have earned a grade of _____ in this

course. *If we disagree, let's get together with our paperwork and resolve*

our differences.

_____   _____
         Teacher Signature   *Date*

Activity #4

Concurrent Evaluation of Behaviors

Getting on the Road

The Quality School Teacher by William Glasser explains concurrent evaluation of content material. In addition to Glasser's suggestions, I find it helpful to co-verify student behaviors and keep a record of my information. The student and I gather information about his or her behaviors on the same day, in the same way, using the same instrument. When students have worked with each other often enough to trust each other, I may also ask another student (in the same cooperative learning group) for his or her perceptions. Seeing ourselves as others see us can be a powerful tool. It can help students reorganize their perceptions about their behaviors and make good choices about effective behaviors the next time they find themselves in a similar situation.

My favorite tool for this job is a list of observable indicators of the behaviors I want to observe accompanied by a Likert scale—a rating scale—for those indicators. It is easy to use and easy for students and parents to understand. I know the student and I are looking for information about the same behaviors at the same time, so there will be no arguing or excusing later on, for example, "You never told me what you were looking for!" or "That's not fair! I focused on one thing while you looked at another!" I hand out copies of the checklists and discuss their use with the whole class early in the year to lay the groundwork for later co-verification.

Cruising the Road

1. This kind of observation checklist can be used almost any time. I find it easiest to focus on one particular student when the class is working in cooperative learning groups.

2. Approach the student you will be observing. Give the student a copy of the observation checklist (behaviors plus Likert scale, found at the end of this section) and explain the obser-

vation/concurrent assessment process. Tell the student, "I will record my perceptions of your behaviors at some later time. Please record your perceptions at the same time. Then we will get together and compare perceptions. If our perceptions do not match, we will discuss possible reasons for those differences. You may choose to make notes about the behaviors to help you remember the reasons for your perceptions. I will probably be doing just that." Ask the student if he or she has any questions about the process. Then move away and begin observing as soon as the student begins the assigned activity.

3. Fill in your copy of the checklist at the time you told the student you would. You may also choose to remind the student to fill in his or her copy of the checklist.

4. I usually observe a few different students during one class period. I give them all their checklists before they start the activity with their cooperative learning groups—that way I do not take them away from their groups during the activity. I also tell them when I will be observing them.

5. The last few minutes of the class period, meet with each student individually to share perceptions. When I do this, I find that most of the time, our perceptions are very close. Occasionally we are very different. I always take time to discuss those differences with students, and those are the times when anecdotal notes are the most helpful. If a student says, "But I was prepared to help the group!," it helps if I can say, "But I saw that you came to class without your books today. If you didn't bring your materials to class, is that what you see as being prepared to help the group?" The student might then say, "Lisa had my book and notes with her. I loaned them to her so that she could catch up on the notes that she missed when she was sick."

6. Sign the student's copy of the checklist; have the student sign yours. Keep your own checklist; tell the student to keep his or hers as part of the grade paper trail.

7. I find that I can observe each student at least three times during a nine-week grading period using the short observation checklists that are included at the end of this chapter. My paper trail is very useful when it is time to figure out grades or

In this activity, students and teacher use their **interpersonal/ social** intelligence to discuss observations of behaviors. Students use their **intrapersonal/ introspective** intelligence to self-evaluate their own behaviors.

when I need information about behaviors for a conference with a parent or administrator.

8. I ask students to observe each other and share perceptions only after the class has agreed to take that step. Students bring a lot of baggage to class with them—and some of that baggage contains negative feelings and perceptions about some of their classmates. I do not want them to feel that a classmate perceives them unfavorably because, "He never liked me!"

Stopping to Think

Using checklists to co-verify or concurrently assess use of behaviors helps students and teachers focus on the same actions at the same time. This tool helps students feel that the observation is objective. Students self-evaluate and are always given the opportunity to discuss perceptions before the checklist is signed. That lessens the feeling that the student is being judged by the teacher and is unjustly blamed or accused of using ineffective, irresponsible behaviors. Using this tool, discussion of behavior is no longer your word against theirs. A record of behaviors exists—a record that was mutually created and mutually agreed upon. Self-evaluation helps students reevaluate their behaviors and their effectiveness. I like this tool a lot and use it a lot!

  IRI/Skylight Training and Publishing, Inc.

Student: _____   **RESPONSIBLE BEHAVIORS**

Date: _____

Observable Indicators	Not Yet 0	So-So 3	You Bet! 5
Comes to class on time, prepared, and focused			
Knows and follows the classroom rules			
Uses responsible behaviors (helps him- or herself but does not hurt others)			
Corrects behaviors quickly (avoids excusing or blaming)			
Encourages classmates and teachers (uses "put-ups," not putdowns)			

■ ■

Student: _____   **RESPONSIBLE BEHAVIORS**

Date: _____

Observable Indicators	Not Yet 0	So-So 3	You Bet! 5
Comes to class on time, prepared, and focused			
Knows and follows the classroom rules			
Uses responsible behaviors (helps him- or herself but does not hurt others)			
Corrects behaviors quickly (avoids excusing or blaming)			
Encourages classmates and teachers (uses "put-ups," not putdowns)			

■ ■

Student: _____   **RESPONSIBLE BEHAVIORS**

Date: _____

Observable Indicators	Not Yet 0	So-So 3	You Bet! 5
Comes to class on time, prepared, and focused			
Knows and follows the classroom rules			
Uses responsible behaviors (helps him- or herself but does not hurt others)			
Corrects behaviors quickly (avoids excusing or blaming)			
Encourages classmates and teachers (uses "put-ups," not putdowns)			

Student: _____   "GOOD STUDENT" BEHAVIORS

Date: _____

Observable Indicators	Not Yet 0	So-So 3	You Bet! 5
Comes to class prepared			
Focuses on lesson/task			
Is in class at least 90% of the time			
Listens to speaker(s) attentively and actively			
Keeps detailed log/journal/notebook			

■■■

Student: _____   "GOOD STUDENT" BEHAVIORS

Date: _____

Observable Indicators	Not Yet 0	So-So 3	You Bet! 5
Comes to class prepared			
Focuses on lesson/task			
Is in class at least 90% of the time			
Listens to speaker(s) attentively and actively			
Keeps detailed log/journal/notebook			

■■■

Student: _____   "GOOD STUDENT" BEHAVIORS

Date: _____

Observable Indicators	Not Yet 0	So-So 3	You Bet! 5
Comes to class prepared			
Focuses on lesson/task			
Is in class at least 90% of the time			
Listens to speaker(s) attentively and actively			
Keeps detailed log/journal/notebook			

IRI/Skylight Training and Publishing, Inc.

Student: _____   **THOUGHTFUL BEHAVIORS**

Date: _____

Observable Indicators	Not Yet 0	So-So 3	You Bet! 5
Asks good questions			
"Links" with prior knowledge			
Describes learnings in words and pictures			
Does quality work			
Transfers learnings to "real life"			

■■

Student: _____   **THOUGHTFUL BEHAVIORS**

Date: _____

Observable Indicators	Not Yet 0	So-So 3	You Bet! 5
Asks good questions			
"Links" with prior knowledge			
Describes learnings in words and pictures			
Does quality work			
Transfers learnings to "real life"			

■■

Student: _____   **THOUGHTFUL BEHAVIORS**

Date: _____

Observable Indicators	Not Yet 0	So-So 3	You Bet! 5
Asks good questions			
"Links" with prior knowledge			
Describes learnings in words and pictures			
Does quality work			
Transfers learnings to "real life"			

Student: _____   TEAMWORK ASSESSMENT

Date: _____

Observable Indicators	Not Yet 0	So-So 3	You Bet! 5
"Stays home"			
Helps with task/Does his or her fair share			
Encourages team to persist			
Invites teammates to participates			
Celebrates success with teammates			

■■

Student: _____   TEAMWORK ASSESSMENT

Date: _____

Observable Indicators	Not Yet 0	So-So 3	You Bet! 5
"Stays home"			
Helps with task/Does his or her fair share			
Encourages team to persist			
Invites teammates to participates			
Celebrates success with teammates			

■■

Student: _____   TEAMWORK ASSESSMENT

Date: _____

Observable Indicators	Not Yet 0	So-So 3	You Bet! 5
"Stays home"			
Helps with task/Does his or her fair share			
Encourages team to persist			
Invites teammates to participates			
Celebrates success with teammates			

IRI/Skylight Training and Publishing, Inc.

Quality is a **Journey**
IT IS NOT A DESTINATION

Quality is a **Vision**
IT IS NOT A MOUNTED PHOTO

Quality **Expands**
IT IS NOT BOXED OR BOUND

Quality is **Dynamic**
IT IS NOT STATIC OR FIXED

Quality is **Internal & Personal**
IT IS NOT DEFINED BY OTHERS

Quality is the **Ultimate Quest**

IRI/Skylight Training and Publishing, Inc.

Bibliography

Bellanca, J. 1990. *The cooperative think tank*. Palatine, Ill.: IRI/Skylight Training and Publishing.

Bellanca, J., and R. Fogarty. 1986. *Catch them thinking: A handbook of classroom strategies*. Palatine, Ill.: IRI/Skylight Training and Publishing.

———. 1990. *Blueprints for thinking in the cooperative classroom*. Palatine, Ill.: IRI/Skylight Training and Publishing.

Bishop, J. H. 1992. Why U. S. students need incentives to learn. *Educational Leadership* 49 (6): 15–18.

Blankenstein, A. M. 1992. Lessons from enlightened corporations. *Educational Leadership* 49 (6): 71–75.

Boffey, D. B. 1993. *Reinventing yourself: A control theory approach to becoming the person you want to be*. Chapel Hill: New View Publications.

Bonstingl, J. J. 1992. The total quality classroom. *Educational Leadership* 49 (6): 66–70.

Burke, K. 1992. *What to do with the kid who...: Developing cooperation, self-discipline, and responsibility in the classroom*. Palatine, Ill.: IRI/Skylight Training and Publishing.

———. 1993. *The mindful school: How to assess authentic learning*. Palatine, Ill.: IRI/Skylight Training and Publishing.

Chapman, C. 1993. *If the shoe fits...: How to develop multiple intelligences in the classroom*. Palatine, Ill.: IRI/Skylight Training and Publishing.

Costa, A. L. 1991. *The school as a home for the mind*. Palatine, Ill.: IRI/Skylight Training and Publishing.

Crawford, D., R. Badine, and R. Hoglund. 1994. *The school for quality learning: Managing the school and classroom the Deming way*. Chapel Hill: New View Publications.

Deming, W. E. 1988. *Out of the crisis*. Cambridge: Massachusetts Institute of Technology.

Fogarty, R., and J. Bellanca. 1989. *Patterns for thinking: Patterns for transfer*. Palatine, Ill.: IRI/Skylight Training and Publishing.

Gardner, H. 1983. *Frames of mind: The theory of multiple intelligences*. New York: HarperCollins Publishers.

————. 1993. *Multiple intelligences: The theory in practice*. New York: HarperCollins Publishers.

Glasser, W. 1984. *Control theory*. New York: HarperCollins Publishers.

————. 1986. *Control theory in the classroom*. New York: HarperCollins.

————. 1992. *The quality school*. New York: HarperCollins.

————. 1993. *The quality school teacher*. New York: HarperCollins.

————. 1995. *The quality school training program, bulletin # 24: Intelligence and outcomes*. Chatsworth, Calif.: The Institute for CT/RT & QM.

Goodlad, J. I. 1984. *A place called school*. New York: McGraw Hill.

Gossen, D. C. 1993. *Restitution: Restructuring school discipline*. Chapel Hill: New View Publications.

Gossen, D., and J. Anderson. 1995. *Creating the conditions: Leadership for quality schools*. Chapel Hill: New View Publications.

Jalongo, M. R. 1992. Teachers' stories: Our ways of knowing. *Educational Leadership* 49 (7): 68–73.

Johnson, D. W., R. T. Johnson, and E. J. Holubec. 1988. *Advanced cooperative learning*. Edina, Minn.: Interaction Book Company.

————. 1988. *Cooperation in the classroom*. Edina, Minn.: Interaction Book Company.

Kohn, A. 1993. *Punished by rewards*. New York: Houghton Mifflin Company.

Linn, R. L., and S. B. Dunbar. 1990. The nation's report card goes home. *Phi Delta Kappan* 72 (2): 127–33.

Mamchur, C. 1990. But . . . the curriculum. *Phi Delta Kappan* 71 (8): 634–37.

Newmann, F. M. 1991. Linking restructuring to authentic student achievement. *Phi Delta Kappan* 73 (6): 458–63.

Packer, A. H. 1992. Taking action on the SCANS report. *Educational Leadership* 49 (6): 27–31.

van DeWeghe, R. 1992. What teachers learn from "kid watching." *Educational Leadership* 94 (7): 49–52.

Wiggins, Grant. 1989. Teaching to the (authentic) test. *Educational Leadership* 46 (7): 41–47.

Williams, R. B. 1993. *More than 50 ways to build team consensus*. Palatine, Ill.: IRI/Skylight Training and Publishing.

IRI/Skylight Training and Publishing, Inc.

Learn from Our Books *and* from Our Authors!

Bring Our Author/Trainers to Your District

At IRI/SkyLight, we have assembled a unique team of outstanding author/trainers with international reputations for quality work. Each has designed high-impact programs that translate powerful new research into successful learning strategies for every student. We design each program to fit your school's or district's special needs.

Training Programs

IRI/SkyLight's training programs extend the renewal process by helping educators move from content-centered to mind-centered classrooms. In our highly interactive workshops, participants learn foundational, research-based information and teaching strategies in an instructional area that they can immediately transfer to the classroom setting. With IRI/SkyLight's specially prepared materials, participants learn how to teach their students to learn for a lifetime.

Network for Systemic Change

Through a partnership with Phi Delta Kappa, IRI/SkyLight offers a Network for site-based systemic change: *The Network of Mindful Schools.* The Network is designed to promote systemic school change as possible and practical when starting with a renewed vision that centers on *what* and *how* each student learns. To help accomplish this goal, Network consultants work with member schools to develop an annual tactical plan and then implement that plan at the classroom level.

Training of Trainers

The Training of Trainers programs train your best teachers, those who provide the highest quality instruction, to coach other teachers. This not only increases the number of teachers you can afford to train in each program, but also increases the amount of coaching and follow-up that each teacher can receive from a resident expert. Our Training of Trainers programs will help you make a systemic improvement in your staff development program.

To receive a FREE COPY of the IRI/SkyLight catalog or more information about trainings offered through IRI/SkyLight, contact **CLIENT SERVICES** at

TRAINING AND PUBLISHING, INC.
2626 S. Clearbrook Dr., Arlington Heights, IL 60005
800-348-4474 • 847-290-6600 • FAX 847-290-6609

There are
one-story intellects,
two-story intellects, and three-story
intellects with skylights. All fact collectors, who
have no aim beyond their facts, are one-story men. Two-story men
compare, reason, generalize, using the labors of the fact collectors as
well as their own. Three-story men idealize, imagine,
predict—their best illumination comes from
above, through the skylight.
—*Oliver Wendell*
Holmes